BLACK HILLS

MYTHS & LEGENDS

THE TRUE STORIES BEHIND HISTORY'S MYSTERIES

T. D. GRIFFITH

Globe
Pequot

Guilford, Connecticut

Globe Pequot

An imprint of The Rowman & Littlefield Publishing Group, Inc.
4501 Forbes Blvd., Ste. 200
Lanham, MD 20706
www.rowman.com

Distributed by NATIONAL BOOK NETWORK

Copyright © 2020 The Rowman & Littlefield Publishing Group, Inc.
Map by Melissa Baker © The Rowman & Littlefield Publishing Group, Inc.

All rights reserved. No part of this book may be reproduced in any form or by any electronic or mechanical means, including information storage and retrieval systems, without written permission from the publisher, except by a reviewer who may quote passages in a review.

British Library Cataloguing in Publication Information available
Library of Congress Control Number: 2019957577

ISBN 978-1-4930-4059-9 (paper : alk. paper)
ISBN 978-1-4930-4060-5 (electronic)

∞™ The paper used in this publication meets the minimum requirements of American National Standard for Information Sciences—Permanence of Paper for Printed Library Materials, ANSI/NISO Z39.48-1992

Contents

Acknowledgments v
Introduction vii
Chapter 1: Where the Big Boys Are Buried 1
Chapter 2: The Ghost of Seth Bullock,
　　　　　　Deadwood's First Lawman 10
Chapter 3: Preacher Smith's Early Demise 19
Chapter 4: Did Deadwood's Brothels Spawn the Term
　　　　　　"Cathouse"? 28
Chapter 5: Crazy Horse: Our Strange Man 37
Chapter 6: The Thoen Stone—Fact or Fraud? 50
Chapter 7: Lame Johnny and the Lost Gold 57
Chapter 8: Chief Two Sticks's Departure 70
Chapter 9: The Ghost of W. E. Adams 85
Chapter 10: The Underground Wilderness 100
Chapter 11: An Unsolved Murder 107
Chapter 12: The Jackalope: South Dakota's Scariest Rabbit 118
Chapter 13: Gutzon Borglum: One Man's Mountain 123
Chapter 14: "Jackson"—Deadwood's Mystery Man 137

Bibliography 145
Index 152
About the Author 159

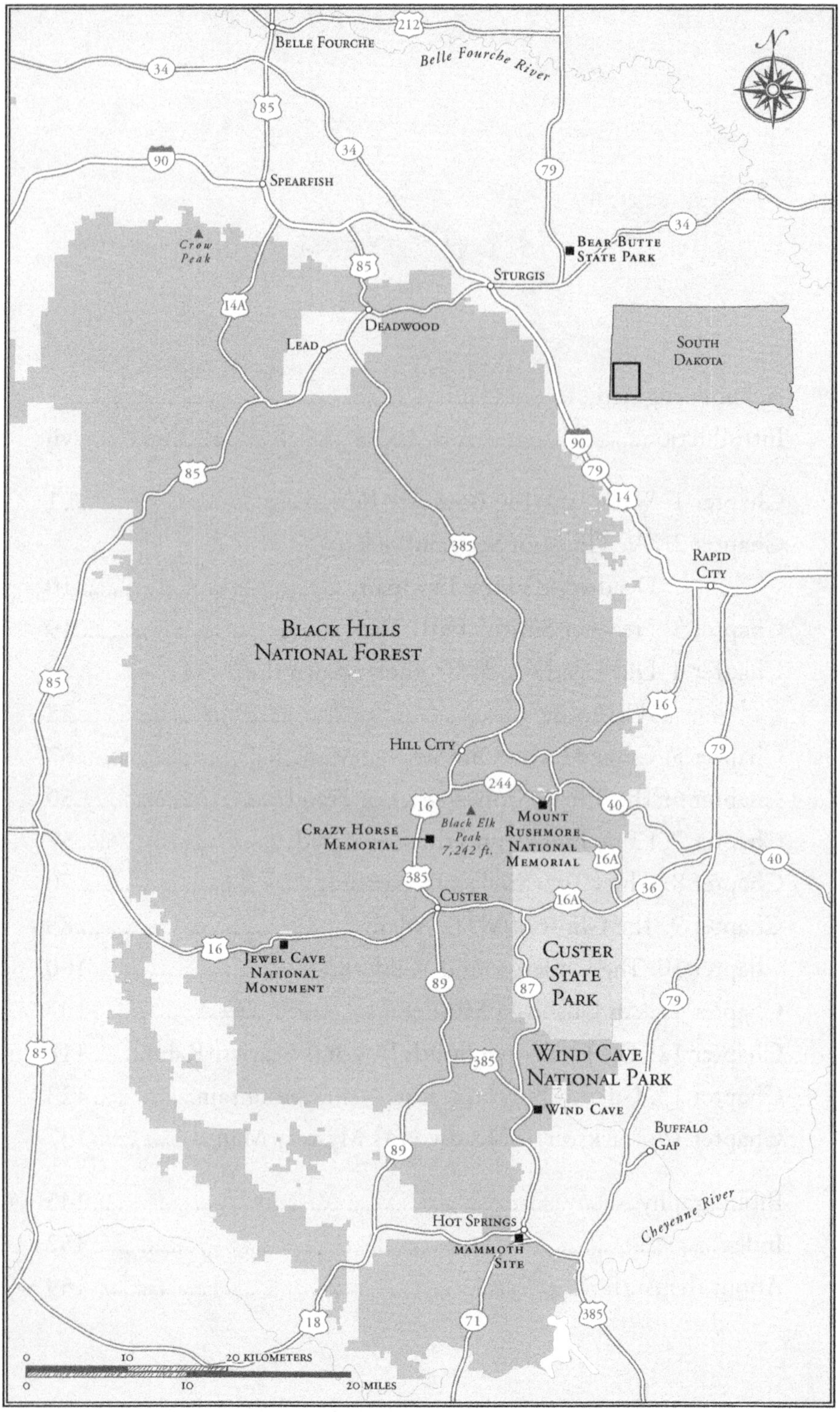

Belle Fourche
Belle Fourche River
Spearfish
Crow Peak
Bear Butte State Park
Sturgis
Deadwood
Lead
South Dakota
Rapid City
Black Hills National Forest
Hill City
Crazy Horse Memorial
Black Elk Peak 7,242 ft.
Mount Rushmore National Memorial
Custer
Jewel Cave National Monument
Custer State Park
Wind Cave National Park
Wind Cave
Buffalo Gap
Cheyenne River
Hot Springs
Mammoth Site
0 10 20 Kilometers
0 10 20 Miles
212
34
85
90
79
14A
14
385
16
16A
244
40
36
89
87
71
18

Acknowledgments

Writers of historical nonfiction are, by necessity, indebted to all of those authors, historians, newspaper reporters, librarians, and documentarians who came before. Their work admittedly, at times, is imperfect, but decades after they've performed their final keystroke, the work that remains may be all we have to describe what happened in the long-distant past.

In producing *Black Hills Myths and Legends*, I am beholden to so many individuals and institutions that have kept history alive by what they left behind. Readers will find references to their work in the manuscript and bibliography, but what they will not find is, in many cases, the friendships that were borne by a mutual love of history, tall tales, and the solitary craft of writing.

My profound thanks to the late writers and friends Rex Alan Smith, whose *The Carving of Mount Rushmore* remains the seminal work about the colossal carving, and Watson Parker, whose *Deadwood: The Golden Years* remains as poignant, well researched, and witty as when it was published in 1981.

Appreciation is also due Carolyn Weber, Rose Speirs, and Hannah Marshall of Deadwood History Inc., which not only operates all of the town's museums, but maintains an exceptional trove of photographs, maps, and memorabilia tied to its rich history and colorful characters. Likewise, thank-yous are owed to Deadwood historic preservation officer Kevin Kuchebecker and archivist Mike Runge for their early help in identifying many of the myths and legends found in this book.

My gratitude to those special people who strive to tell a story of uniqueness found throughout the Black Hills, including Dr. James Mead and Bethany Cook at The Mammoth Site; Jadwiga Ziolkowski and Krista Knapp at Crazy Horse Memorial; my friend Tom Farrell, chief of interpretation at Wind Cave National Park; Mary Kopco, former director of the Adams Museum; and the staff, past and present, at the Bullock Hotel.

Kudos to my editor Courtney Oppel at Rowman & Littlefield, without whose guidance, patience, and persistence this work would never have been completed.

Special credit is extended to my stepson, Dustin Floyd, with whom I've co-authored several books and published *Deadwood Magazine* for nearly a decade. His research, writing, and technical abilities are enviable. And finally, thanks to my loving wife, Nyla, who knows she will have my undivided attention until the next book project comes along.

Introduction

The Black Hills of South Dakota are an ancient million-acre marvel in the middle of America filled with history, mystery, myth, and legend.

As a young boy, I was captivated by the place where my grandparents homesteaded. They ran a small dairy operation on what was then the outskirts of Rapid City, hugging the eastern flank of what the Lakota named *Paha Sapa*, literally Hills Black. Along the way, I reveled in their stories, as well as my mother's accounts of her youth on the ranch where they finally got electricity when she was in the eleventh grade. And, I watched in awe as cowboys and real Native Americans walked the downtown streets.

When my grandfather took his thirteen grandkids on an annual pilgrimage to Mount Rushmore National Memorial for breakfast with the presidents, a grand adventure, the four giant carvings were not only larger than life, they were as big as the world could get.

A half-century later, I'm still learning about this remarkable region that was the last portion of the Lower 48 to even be mapped. So old is this place, yet so young in terms of human existence. To paraphrase my late friend, author Rex Alan Smith, in a geologic context, the Black Hills were taller than the Rockies when the Himalayas were a reedy swamp.

While the majority of this tome explores the misdeeds of early-day outlaws, hopeful prospectors, strong-jawed lawmen, and a few ghosts who still refuse to go away, so too does it survey a remarkable bone bed discovered in 1974, the world's largest final resting place of six-metric-ton beasts that once roamed this land, and a legendary Lakota leader who fought the good fight, but could never reclaim a vanishing landscape.

We'll delve into the exploits and untimely demise of a frontier street preacher who some say died at the hand of a hired gun paid by saloon and brothel owners who thought he was bad for business in Deadwood's earliest days. And, we'll give a glance at an educated horse thief turned gold-coach robber whose millions in plunder may still be stashed somewhere in the Black Hills.

Finally, we'll get down and dirty in a vast underground wilderness beneath this alpine oasis which scientists are only beginning to understand, and which may hold the largest caves on earth, and investigate an etched sandstone slab that may be evidence that white men searched the Hills decades before General George Armstrong Custer ever arrived on the scene.

So, sit back, imagine, and savor some history and mystery with *Black Hills Myths and Legends*.

Chapter 1

Where the Big Boys Are Buried

While the vast majority of myths, mysteries, and legends tied to the Black Hills trace their origins to the arrival of gold-hungry prospectors in the latter part of the nineteenth century, one tantalizing tale began nearly two hundred thousand years ago.

Remarkably, it wasn't discovered until 1974.

On that warm June day, heavy equipment operator George Hanson was at the controls of a grader working to level a small hill on the southwest side of Hot Springs in the southern Black Hills in preparation for a housing development being undertaken by the land owner, Phil Anderson.

As Hanson moved the blade of his grader through the dirt, he noticed it had struck something that appeared white in the bright sunlight. Stepping down from his equipment to get a closer look, Hanson discovered a seven-foot-long tusk that appeared to have been sliced in half. Surrounding it in the newly turned earth were several smaller bones.

The startling discovery not only surprised Hanson, but has been captivating scientists from around the world ever since. For Hanson had not only discovered the massive tusk of one of the largest animals to ever roam the planet, he had accidentally stumbled on what would become the largest graveyard of woolly and Columbian mammoths in one location ever found on earth.

To their enduring credit, Hanson and Anderson did not simply cover their "tracks" and continue with site preparations for the new housing complex. Instead, Anderson reached out to three of South Dakota's universities and colleges, as well as another institution of higher learning in Nebraska, to gauge their interest. None of those academies determined that there was any relevance to the find, let alone expressed a desire to travel to the far-flung Black Hills to examine what had just been unearthed in Hot Springs.

While Anderson was tethered to his telephone, excitedly explaining the giant tusk that had been laid bare on his land, Hanson was eager to know more and took several of the bones to his son, Dan, who had taken college courses in archaeology and geology. The young man quickly grasped the importance of the find and contacted his former professor, Dr. Larry Agenbroad at Nebraska's Chadron State College. Dr. Agenbroad happened to be in southeastern Arizona at the time, excavating a site where mammoths had been hunted and killed.

Concerned, the younger Hanson stood guard at the Hot Springs site, keeping a twenty-four-hour vigil until Dr. Agenbroad and his crew could arrive. When Agenbroad first glanced at the number of bones unearthed by the bulldozer, he estimated there were four to six mammoths in evidence. But, from his vast experience uncovering the world's paleontological mysteries, he knew there had to be more.

Pressed for time and with an outstanding commitment at the Hudson-Meng Bison kill site near Crawford, Nebraska, Agenbroad asked his colleague, Dr. Jim Mead, and several members of his Arizona dig crew, to spend ten days salvaging and stabilizing the bones, tusks, teeth, and skull fragments that had been, for the first time in more than one hundred thousand years, exposed to sunlight.

Meanwhile Anderson, who owned the land on which the find had been made, generously offered to halt his housing project until the crew had a better handle on what was actually there. The decision proved prescient, for in that span of less than two weeks, investigators uncovered an unprecedented collection of specimens, warranting further study.

Over the ensuing years, Agenbroad and Mead would return to the site each summer with a cadre of volunteer students to further excavate the open-air site. After removing the covering from the year before, this collection of dedicated scientists would spend weeks digging deeper into the mystery of this mammoth site. By the end of the summer of 1975, Agenbroad, Mead, and their team of volunteer scholars had exposed a complete skull with tusks intact. Then, as the leaves turned color that fall and the temperatures cooled, they covered it all up with dirt.

Simultaneously, as the summer excavation came to a close, Anderson realized his fourteen acres of land might prove more valuable as a place to study the ancient past than as another plot for new residences. Through Anderson's generosity and wide community support, The Mammoth Site of Hot Springs became South

Dakota's newest nonprofit organization and a place where the world would soon come to realize the big boys were buried.

Thousands of years ago, as the Ice Age changed the climate of the southern Black Hills and much of the United States, massive Columbian and woolly mammoths roamed the range in search of food and warmth. As The Mammoth Site shows, some of them stayed and became permanent residents.

Today, The Mammoth Site has changed drastically from the remote and arid hillside Drs. Agenbroad and Mead first encountered in 1974. A massive modern building encloses the site, complete with bone preparation areas, a museum, and a bookstore that is extremely popular with scientists who visit from all corners of the globe. More than one hundred thousand annual visitors, including numerous school groups, take an audio tour of the bone bed and stand next to replicas of the largest mammals to ever leave their footprints on the planet.

To date, fifty-eight Columbian and three woolly mammoths have been unearthed, all left *in situ* so scientists may consider their placement and their remains as they have rested for millennia. Amazingly, all of the enormous beasts thus far revealed have been male.

In addition, more than eighty other species have been discovered, including a camel, llama, coyotes, three fish, and a vast array of rodents ranging from prairie dogs and gophers to weasels.

But new discoveries occur virtually every year, leaving scientists to wonder: What really is down there?

For instance, in 2018 diggers uncovered the fossil of a second giant short-faced bear found at The Mammoth Site. That's

Volunteers carefully uncover the remains of giant beasts that once roamed the earth in the "bone bed" of The Mammoth Site in Hot Springs, South Dakota. To date, fifty-eight Columbian and three woolly mammoths have been discovered, as well as eighty other species, including the giant short-faced bear.

significant because the ferocious giant short-faced bear made a full-grown grizzly look like a docile panda.

More interestingly, after a two-year study completed in 2018, scientists received a mammoth surprise when they learned the site was actually more than five times older than originally thought.

As initially envisioned, about twenty-six thousand years ago, as the earth entered the Ice Age and the climate cooled, mammoths and other species were attracted to the warm waters of this giant, slippery-sided sinkhole situated on the southwestern flank of the Black Hills. Those same thermal waters helped vegetation grow along the sinkhole's perimeters, providing a magnet for hungry critters.

Over hundreds if not thousands of years during the Pleistocene (Ice Age) era, curious mammoths and other animals would stumble upon the sinkhole, slip down a slippery slope, and, unable to extricate themselves, over the succeeding days or weeks, either drown or die of exhaustion or starvation. As their remains settled to the bottom of the pit, the next unfortunate mammoth would fall in, stir up the pot of mud, blood, dirt, and vegetation, and cover the previous mammoth with a comfortable cloak of silt. Evidence suggests this went on for thousands of years.

Then, due to changes in the earth's topography over eons, the giant sinkhole eventually dried up and, aided by up-thrusts and sedimentation, became a small hill flanking the granite mountains of the Black Hills, as the land around it eroded.

Initially, geochemical analysis that included radiocarbon dating indicated that the sinkhole was full of warm water and struggling mammoths about twenty-six thousand years ago. But, as the number of mammoths discovered grew over the decades and technology advanced, in 2016, Dr. Mead decided to take a closer look at assessing the precise age of the sinkhole and its inhabitants by employing a new technique.

He enlisted Dr. Steve Holen, a Mammoth Site science associate and board member who had been collaborating with a colleague, Dr. Shannon A. Mahan of the US Geological Survey in Denver, for a number of years. The duo had been using OSL (Optically Stimulated Luminescence) in attempting to date some of Holen's mammoth sites in Nebraska and around the region. Consequently, in January 2016, a group assembled at The Mammoth Site and took a number of samples of sediments to analyze.

The crew did core drilling and used chisels, hammers, and an electric saw to obtain sediment samples that were then analyzed using a portable gamma spectrometer. Following an extended laboratory analysis, Dr. Mead and his team termed the results, "A nice shocker."

When they learned the sinkhole actually dated back one hundred forty thousand to one hundred ninety thousand years, far older than originally believed, Mead said he felt enlightened. The researchers knew that one hundred forty thousand years ago, the climate of the earth was heading into an extremely warm interglacial period "warmer than what we are in today—at this time South Dakota and elsewhere was coming out of a period of massive glaciers covering all of Canada and much of northern-most USA," Mead told the media at the time. "We are still learning a lot about the Mammoth Site sinkhole and its sixty-plus mammoths."

Over the years, The Mammoth Site has received its share of accolades. The active paleontological dig site and accredited museum was named the number one museum in South Dakota by *USA Today*, and the coolest museum in South Dakota by *The Discoverer Blog*. The exceptional Hot Springs attraction, which is open year-round, offers guided tours, summer programs for children, exhibits, and hands-on displays.

And much more is likely to be studied and discovered.

Scientists have long pondered why all of the sinkhole's dead inhabitants were males. Some animal behavioralists have since surmised that mammoth mannerisms may have echoed today's elephant herds, which practice a matriarchal society. As the dominant male mammoths would check out the slick sides of the sinkhole,

A life-sized replica of a mammoth greets guests at The Mammoth Site in Hot Springs, South Dakota. The nonprofit attraction is home to the largest concentration of Columbian and woolly mammoths found anywhere on the planet.

the females would stand back and watch attentively, they contend. When the males eventually fell in and never reappeared, perhaps the females decided this really wasn't the place for them.

Joe Muller, who served as business manager and chief operating officer for The Mammoth Site for three decades, still wonders why a bison fossil has never been found amongst the mammoths. Yet, says Muller, from snails to mammoths, The Mammoth Site continues to reveal nature's ancient riddles about water temperatures over time, extinction, and climate change.

And spokeswoman Bethany Cook claims she is still entranced each day by this singular place, which ranks among the most amazing educational and paleontological sites in the world. Though it has slowly divulged its secrets over the past half-century, Cook contends The Mammoth Site may have more confidences to reveal.

"We've gone down forty to forty-five feet, but what remains under what we discovered so far?" she asked. "Will we find something different? We don't know. Will we find other species we haven't seen yet or will we find a female mammoth? There are so many mysteries that remain."

Chapter 2

The Ghost of Seth Bullock, Deadwood's First Lawman

Long and lean, with a mean mustache meant to complement his holstered six-gun and western attire, Seth Bullock cut a swath as he sauntered down Deadwood's muddy Main Street in the 1870s. And, some say he still does.

Among the first to arrive in the Black Hills for America's last great gold rush in 1876, Bullock wasn't hell-bent on working a claim or standing knee-deep in a cold stream all day, trying to eke out a few spots of color in his pan. No, this Canadian-turned-Montanan-turned-Dakotan would let the prospectors turn their efforts into a hard-earned sack of gold dust while selling them everything they needed to build a life in the Black Hills.

An extremely successful merchant, the former soldier in the Spanish-American War known as Bullock also became close friends with President Theodore Roosevelt who, afraid his sons would become eastern dandies, would send his boys to Bullock for a summer where he would teach them to build a fire, shoot a gun, and take care of their horse before they took care of themselves.

The Canadian-born Bullock had previously lived in Montana, where he served in the territorial legislature. Following the scent of gold in the Black Hills, Bullock arrived in Deadwood with his business partner, Sol Star, just a couple of days before Wild Bill Hickok was slain by a no-account drifter named Crooked Nose Jack McCall.

But Hickok's death wasn't an anomaly in the community's infancy, when some claimed there was a death a day from unnatural causes. In addition to numerous instances of claim-jumping that frequently concluded at the bad end of a smoking six-gun, other official causes of death listed by the few doctors in town at the time included "hit by a falling body," "ate a dozen hard-boiled eggs," "gored by a buffalo," and "shot sparking another man's wife." Eventually, Deadwood's founding fathers turned to the tall former Montana sheriff with steel gray eyes, a stern man not easily intimidated by rabble-rousers or drunken miners.

Although he unofficially was as an early-day lawman for the town, in 1877, a year after his arrival, Bullock served a brief stint as Deadwood's sheriff. It was during that time that a heartbroken Teddy Roosevelt, in the wake of the deaths of both his mother and wife on the same day, escaped to the Badlands of North Dakota. The two met up on the Dakota Territory plains when the future president was bringing a horse-thief known as Crazy Steve to Deadwood for trial.

Bullock would later be named a captain of Troop A of Grisby's cowboy regiment, but was confined to training in Louisiana

One of Deadwood's first residents and its first marshal, Seth Bullock was an entrepreneur and personal friend of President Theodore Roosevelt. This photograph of Bullock was taken in 1882.

COURTESY DEADWOOD HISTORY INC., ADAMS MUSEUM COLLECTION

when Roosevelt made his famous charge up San Juan Hill. Nonetheless, the Oyster Bay Roosevelt and the Dakota cowboy would remain lifelong friends. In fact, Roosevelt would come to refer to Bullock as "my ideal typical American."

By 1900, Vice President Roosevelt convinced President William McKinley to name Bullock the first supervisor of Black Hills National Forest. In 1905, Roosevelt appointed him US marshal, a position reconfirmed by President William Howard Taft and for a year under President Woodrow Wilson.

The late historian Watson Parker noted that Bullock performed his lawman's duties with a determined professionalism that rarely ended in gunfire, because the western lawman, as his son would later attest, "could outstare a mad cobra or a rogue elephant."

"He never actually found it necessary to kill anybody in the performance of his varied duties, but he was well-prepared to use the requisite amount of force even if it involved blowing off the top of the skull of some recalcitrant malefactor," Parker wrote. "Bullock's forceful demeanor enabled him to carry out his duties with a minimum of violence, for a single glance into his steely eyes convinced most criminals that this was not a man with whom they could much prank around."

But Bullock wasn't only concerned with the lawless aspects of the rough and rowdy gold camp. Shortly after arriving in Deadwood in August 1876, he and Star would invest $60,000, a princely sum, in the Deadwood Flouring Mill Co. Over time, Bullock also raised cattle in the Belle Fourche valley and is actually credited with establishing the town of Belle Fourche. He also dabbled in banking, brewing beer, bringing the railroad to Deadwood, and running a wholesale and retail mercantile that sold everything from furniture, hardware, and lamps to silverware and wallpaper.

Strangely, one of the first shipments Bullock and Star received included a large selection of chamber pots "of various shapes and colors," which Bullock auctioned off to needy miners in what Watson surmised, "must have been one of the high points of Black Hills oratory and enterprise."

During the forty-three years Bullock spent in Deadwood, he remained fast friends with Theodore Roosevelt. In addition to helping turn T.R.'s sons "into men" on the open range, Bullock once served as a stern and heavily armed protector for Roosevelt while the latter was campaigning in South Dakota, and later joined a cadre of Roughriders in riding horses down Pennsylvania Avenue during the president's inaugural in Washington, DC.

When Bullock visited Washington, DC, on government business on February 23, 1903, the White House and the *Chicago Tribune* took notice.

"Seth Bullock of South Dakota was the guest of the president at luncheon today, and late in the afternoon went out horseback riding with him," the newspaper reported the following day. The article continued:

> Bullock is chief forest ranger for the Black Hills district and is in Washington on official business with the interior department. When President Roosevelt heard he was in town he sent for him, and they had a fine time today renewing old acquaintance. Bullock was the first marshal of Deadwood, and he has been known as a "bad man with

a gun" ever since the Black Hills excitement of twenty or thirty years ago.

When Mr. Roosevelt made his campaign tour through the west in 1900 Seth Bullock accompanied him through South Dakota. It was rumored that Bryanites were planning to break up the Roosevelt meeting in Deadwood. "Don't you worry," said Seth Bullock to Mr. Roosevelt. "Leave that to me; I'll fix 'em." On the afternoon before the meeting he passed around the word in Deadwood that he would sit on the platform with Roosevelt that evening armed with his six-shooters and that he would kill any person who made a disturbance. Bullock attracted general attention around the White House today. He has a fierce melodrama mustache and wears a sombrero.

Following his presidency, Roosevelt embarked on a weekslong safari in Africa before being wined and dined by European royalty. After countless evenings spent in formal gatherings, Roosevelt wired Bullock in Deadwood, told the marshal that such finery, rich food and fashion, and polite conversation had left him thoroughly bored and asked Bullock to visit him in London. Subsequently, Bullock got on his horse and rode it to Pierre, South Dakota, then took a succession of trains to New York City, where he boarded a ship and sailed the Atlantic to England, all done solely to satisfy a friend.

When the twenty-sixth president of the United States died in 1919, Bullock was deeply saddened by the loss of his lifelong friend. With assistance from some of his well-heeled Deadwood associates,

Bullock had a Friendship Tower constructed just north of town on one of the area's tallest peaks. Dedicated just weeks before Bullock's own death from cancer, Mount Roosevelt was the first memorial in America dedicated to the statesman, politician, conservationist, naturalist, and writer.

Among Bullock's many accomplishments in a varied career was building the Bullock Hotel, which still stands on Main Street. This elegant lodge featured Turkish baths and brass beds and billed itself as among the finest accommodations between Chicago and Denver.

Although Bullock died in the fall of 1919, just a few months after his friend T.R., some claim his ghost never left Deadwood, and to this day his frequent appearances have helped the old hotel gain a ghostly reputation. Some say the marshal remains on duty in what was known as the wildest and wooliest town in the West.

Guests and employees of the fabled hotel have often shared their stories of encounters with Bullock. So many have done so, in fact, that NBC's *Unsolved Mysteries* did an entire segment on those strange interactions in the early 1990s.

For example, guests have checked out of the hotel in the middle of the night after they awoke to find an old cowboy standing in his Stetson and slicker at the end of their bed. In Seth's Cellar, a bar located in the basement of the establishment, on numerous occasions employees have reported that chairs have mysteriously moved with no one in sight.

While conducting a familiarization tour for travel journalists, a South Dakota Tourism guide, ever the skeptic, told the reporters

Although Seth Bullock died a century ago, some say his ghost still haunts his namesake hotel.

about the frequent sightings of Bullock that had occurred at the hotel. That same night, while reading a book in bed in one of the Bullock Hotel's guest rooms, that guide reported that her reading light next to her bed inexplicably extinguished, while a floor lamp across the room simultaneously turned on, making her a believer.

Other strange occurrences include guests and staff feeling a paranormal presence inside rooms and in the hallways of the second and third floor. Some have reported plates and glasses taking flight in the historic hotel's restaurant or being tapped on the shoulder by unseen hands. Lights, appliances, televisions, and even showers have purportedly turned on and off of their own accord.

But perhaps the most unusually strange accounts come from guests who have heard an unseen man call out their names, or simply whistle or hum a tune in the night. Whether truth or conjecture, all agree that the legendary lawman known as Seth Bullock continues to play host at his famous Deadwood hotel.

CHAPTER 3

Preacher Smith's Early Demise

In the ribald and lawless early days of Deadwood, as many as ten thousand merchants, miners, and madams descended on the fabled gold-filled gulch in a matter of weeks, each in search of their private El Dorado.

Some historians contend there was a death a day in the town's infancy, most from unnatural causes. Whiskey flowed freely in Deadwood's countless saloons, where musicians tickled the ivories in the downstairs bars while upstairs girls flaunted their wares in darkened rooms.

In their midst walked the Reverend Henry Weston Smith, a man uninterested in earthly possessions and eager to spread the word of the Lord to those who paid scant regard to Christian living. As the first minister of any denomination in the Black Hills gold rush camps, Preacher Smith, as he came to be known, would proselytize on the streets and in the saloons.

On Sundays, he'd travel to outlying camps to spread the word. One Sunday morning, August 20, 1876, Preacher Smith had done his deed in Deadwood before turning his feet toward Crook City, intent on preaching there. But he never made it.

His lifeless body was found shot through the heart on a ridge a few miles from town, an undelivered sermon still folded neatly in his pocket. Townspeople quickly suspected that Preacher Smith had been ambushed by marauding Indians, fresh from their victory at the Battle of the Little Big Horn.

Still others believed the minister's life had been extinguished by gunmen paid by local saloon-keepers and brothel owners who thought his God-fearing message was bad for business. We may never know.

What we do know is Preacher Smith was born in Ellington, Connecticut, on January 10, 1827. Twenty years later he married, but his wife and young son died just a year into their marriage, leading the young widower to the Lord. By age twenty-three, Smith had become a Methodist minister and began preaching to the faithful throughout Connecticut.

Shortly after he turned thirty-two, Smith took his second wife, Lydia Ann Joslin, and the couple was blessed with four children. The family eventually moved to Massachusetts and when the Civil War broke out, Smith wore blue in fighting for the state's 52nd Infantry. When hostilities eventually ceased with General Robert E. Lee's surrender of the last major Confederate army on April 9, 1865, and having witnessed the carnage of battle, Smith became a doctor.

Though the fate of his family has been lost to time, Smith knew his calling as a minister would serve him well in the raucous and rowdy frontier camps when General George Armstrong

Custer's 1874 expedition into the Black Hills confirmed the presence of gold in ample quantities. The newest gold strike set off a wave of would-be fortune seekers who descended on the Black Hills like locusts.

By the spring of 1876, Smith had joined the entourage of thousands seeking their private El Dorados in the million-acre wilderness standing on the western edge of Dakota Territory. At the time, the region remained the last in the country to even be mapped. But Smith wasn't seeking earthly rewards; rather, he sought a place to spread the gospel to those who needed to hear it most.

During that soggy spring of 1876, Smith must have called on his inner strength and that of a divine power in walking beside a wagon train as it traveled from Cheyenne, Wyoming, to the first settlement in the Black Hills known as Custer City—a distance of some 250 miles. At that early town, it's said Preacher Smith conducted the first church service in the Hills, pontificating to a congregation comprised of thirty men and five women.

After preaching again the following Sunday, Smith received permission from Captain C. V. Gardner to walk alongside his wagon train as it made its way north to the burgeoning gold mining camp being settled in Deadwood Gulch—another fifty-six-mile slog through rough country and pine forests that took three days.

Captain Gardner would later describe the early-day settlement of Deadwood, named for all the downed timber the first miners stumbled upon when they reached the gold-filled gulch, as well as the untruths surrounding the religious man he came to know:

In the years past I have noted in the press many statements regarding incidents connected with the man known as Preacher Smith. Most of them are pure romance. . . . how he used to go into the saloons and pray are pure fiction. I never saw him in a saloon, and I am sure he never was. He preached frequently in Deadwood, generally in front of Bent and Deetken's drug store or in front of my store. . . . in those days the town had 3,000 to 4,000 people, located mostly on one street, and he had no trouble in securing an audience. He was a man about 6 feet tall, with a fine physique and I should say 40 years old. He was very quiet and unassuming in manner. I know nothing of his past life, as he never volunteered to tell me and it was not wise in those days to inquire too closely into a man's antecedents.

Other early-day Deadwood pioneers wrote of Preacher Smith in their memoirs, remembering a man who prospected and worked odd jobs digging ditches or helping at a lumber mill during the week to support his penchant for street-preaching in the open air on Sundays, generally on the muddy and often bloody Main Street of Deadwood. His informal sermons rarely drew a large crowd, but the devoted pioneer preacher would nonetheless stand atop his packing crate and deliver his message while a respectful gathering of townspeople took it in.

Historian and author Watson Parker, who wrote the exceptionally researched account of the fabled town's early days in *Deadwood: The Golden Years*, recounted a story of Calamity Jane Canary listening to one of Smith's street sermons:

PREACHER SMITH'S EARLY DEMISE

It is claimed that Calamity Jane, hearing him preaching, came up, took his hat in her hand and circulated among the congregation, saying, "You sinners, dig down in your pokes now; this old fellow looks as though he were broke and I want to collect about two hundred dollars for him. So limber up, boys." When Smith, instead of at once accepting the money, went on with his sermon, she forced the collection upon him saying, "You damned old fool, take the money first, then proceed with your preaching." If this story isn't true, it ought to be.

But Smith didn't restrict his biblical lessons to the hardworking, hard-drinking crowd of miners, merchants, and prostitutes of Deadwood. After building a primitive cabin, he would sometimes venture out to call on smaller, nearby gold camps such as Gayville, Galena, and Tinton.

But traveling the backcountry trails of the Black Hills in its earliest days was never without danger. Indian war parties scavenged for whatever they could find, while crooks, culprits, and cutthroats would often rob travelers of valuables, then kill them all to prevent a witness from leading them to the gallows on some unfortunate, future date.

Parker wrote that even well-armed and sizeable parties were not immune from attack, particularly in the lawless early days of the mid-1870s.

"All told, some thirty-five to forty incoming pilgrims were killed by Indians during the troubles of 1876, although estimates as high as one hundred were not uncommon," Parker wrote. The respected historian also noted that skittish travelers, wary of what lay over the next rise or in the heart of darkness, were as prone to shoot each other as they were to be attacked by murderous marauders.

Apparently, friends of Preacher Smith warned him against walking alone on his frequent wanderings, worried he would be attacked. When they eventually advised him to carry a gun, Smith reportedly replied, "The Bible is my protection. It has never failed me yet."

On the morning of August 20, 1876, Preacher Smith's Bible failed him. After tacking a note to his cabin door that read, "Gone to Crook City to preach, and if God is willing, will be back at three o'clock," the reverend set out on foot on an eleven-mile trek to the small mining camp located northeast of Deadwood. Though he would never know it, the man of the cloth had already given his last sermon.

Later that afternoon, on a hilltop just a mile or so from downtown Deadwood, a local resident came upon the prone body of Preacher Smith. He had not been robbed, as was customary, and had been shot once (others say twice) in the heart. In his coat pocket was found his final sermon. His body was taken into town for burial.

The next day, Deadwood marshal Seth Bullock reported details of the clergyman's death in a letter sent to the Reverend J. S. Chadwick:

> It becomes my painful duty to inform you that Rev. H. Weston Smith was killed by the Indians yesterday (Sunday)

This drawing, done by an unknown artist, is of the Reverend Henry Weston Smith, the first minister of any denomination to travel to the gold rush camps of the Black Hills in 1876. Just months after his arrival, the lifeless body of Preacher Smith was found a few miles from Deadwood.

a short distance from this place. He had an appointment to preach here in the afternoon, and was on his way from Crook City when a band of Indians overtook him and shot him. His body was not mutilated in any way, and was found in the road a short time after the hellish deed had been done. His death was instantaneous as he was shot through the heart. His funeral occurred today from his home in this town. Everything was done by kind hands, that was possible under the circumstances, and a Christian burial given him. I was not personally acquainted with Mr. Smith, but knew him by reputation, as an earnest worker in his Master's Vineyard. He has preached here on several occasions, and was the only minister in the Hills. He died in the harness and his memory will be always with those who knew him. A letter from you which I found in his home causes me to convey this sad intelligence to you.

In Smith's rites of passage, Bullock also conducted what is believed to be the first Episcopal service ever conducted in Deadwood, and the lawman read from the Book of Common Prayer over the grave of Preacher Smith. Later, Smith's casket would be exhumed and transferred to Mt. Moriah Cemetery where it remains today, just steps away from the final resting places of Wild Bill Hickok and Calamity Jane.

In 1914 the Society of Black Hills Pioneers erected a monument on the Deadwood-Spearfish road, near where Smith's body was found. Due to a highway expansion, a new monument was rededicated near the same spot on August 20, 1995, 119 years to the day of Smith's death.

Although Smith's death was widely attributed to Indians, some believe he may have been killed by common road thieves, although the fact he had not been robbed argued against that theory.

Others thought his death far more sinister, the conspiracy of a group of saloon and brothel owners who feared Smith would convert the sinners of Deadwood to religion and more godly lives. It was noted that Smith's sermons eventually would deprive the saloons, gambling dens, and brothels of considerable income. Of course, the same scheme was put forth after the death of Wild Bill Hickok, a former lawman who some surmised had come to the raucous and ribald town to clean it up.

In the days, weeks, months, and years following the untimely demise of Preacher Smith, Deadwood residents went about their lives, mining gold, building businesses, and raising families. But the townspeople never forgot the first clergyman to come to the Black Hills, and the story of Preacher Smith is still recounted alongside those of its other famous permanent residents, and the identity of his killer is still debated.

His last sermon, found in the pocket of his threadbare coat, is still recited, as is the following poem, evidence of his thoughtfulness and literary prowess.

> *This evening is the first of June,*
> *And snow is falling fast.*
> *The tall pines sigh, howl, and moan,*
> *Responsive to the blast.*
> *The shades of night are gathered 'round;*
> *The fire is burning low,*
> *I sit and watch the dying coals,*
> *And think of long ago.*

Chapter 4

Did Deadwood's Brothels Spawn the Term "Cathouse"?

For more than a century, Deadwood's brothels operated with relative impunity in a wild and wooly town where city officials and law enforcement either ignored the carnal pursuits or simply dismissed them with a wink and a nod.

From the earliest gold rush days of 1876, right up to the May day in 1980 when federal agents finally raided the remaining houses of ill repute and closed them all down, "upstairs girls" ruled the night. During deer hunting season each fall, they even ruled much of the day, kept busy by a line of skin-hungry out-of-towners hoping to scratch a peculiar itch.

Confined primarily to the "badlands" district on the lower end of Main Street, dens of iniquity called the Gem, Green Front, Cricket, Bella Union, and the Melodean plied their trade for decades, often with young women brought in by the proprietor with promises of lucrative waitressing jobs or appreciated appearances on stage for songs and skits. After their arrival by stagecoach, many quickly learned that, in addition to their boss's well-watered whiskey and soggy cigars, they were expected to cadge drinks and sell anything they had to sour-smelling miners, cowpokes, hunters, and beleaguered husbands slyly out for a night on the town.

Historian and author Watson Parker recounted the experience of one small-town girl who stepped foot in Deadwood only to realize that she had walked into a world that she had never contemplated.

"Inez Sexton was one such innocent girl, and when she saw the vile situation that she had got herself into, she announced to Al Swearengen, who by that time owned the Gem, that although her voice was for sale nothing else was, and she stalked out of his low dive in high dudgeon," Parker wrote. "Colonel Cornell, a spectator, loaned her money to put up at a respectable hotel, and a benefit was arranged by the good ladies of the town to provide the escaped songbird with stage fare back home again."

In those early years, many down-on-their-luck prospectors sought their riches from the pokes of more prosperous miners, just as a bevy of prostitutes hungry to meet their quota sold their services to the men with a healthy poke. Indeed, Deadwood was a rich, ribald, and rough place where a wrong turn down an alley could lead a man to conquer his confirmed habit of living, and a roll with the wrong woman could result in a gift that kept on giving.

One anonymous druggist purportedly made $500 per month catering to the medical needs of the prostitutes with medicines and various concoctions intended to prevent, treat, or cure a number of maladies associated with the infectious business. And many a Deadwood doctor augmented his income from office visits with weekly inspections of the upstairs girls largely hidden in the whorehouses.

To this day, a visitor may encounter a local who, as a teen, worked in one of Deadwood's many shops, stores, dispensaries, and mercantiles while the brothels still were in operation. And to this day those former early clerks can recall Monday afternoons, when upstanding local female residents would do anything but be caught seen in a local business.

Determined to maintain a sense of decorum, proper ladies of Deadwood would avoid doing any of their shopping on Monday afternoons, lest they run into those lowly hookers who used that unofficial period to browse and buy all kinds of merchandise, from undergarments and dresses, to soaps, lotions, and other personal necessities.

Likewise, modern-day residents of Deadwood claim it was a cast of faceless characters who gave the town its unwieldy reputation, not Wild Bill Hickok or Calamity Jane—although the latter's propensity to howl at the moon when tipsy is still fondly recalled. And, as most local residents will attest, that same cast of unusual characters, albeit with different names, still inhabits the place.

Historian Parker probably described those early Deadwood days best, writing in 1981:

> Nowadays the people of Deadwood like to claim that it was not the Wild [*sic*] characters, the Wild Bills and Calamity Janes, that gave the town its fame and character, but the zeal with which lives are remembered and the obscurity

In its raucous early years, Deadwood's notorious "badlands district" on the lower end of Main Street was home to numerous saloons, casinos, and brothels, which some called "cathouses." Seen here is the Gem Theater, one of the most infamous dens of iniquity. Driving the buggy on the left is Al Swearengen, owner of the Gem.

with which history cloaks the respectable is a pretty good indication that Deadwood liked its people with the hair on.

Swill Barrel Jimmy, Johnny-Behind-the-Deuce, and the Grasshopper, who walked the streets bawling out obscenities, were the remembered part of Deadwood, and Deadwood took them to its heart. Pancake Bill, Mysterious Jimmy, Bedrock Tom, Happy George, Johnny the Oyster, Club Foot Frank, Cheating Sheely, Laughing Sam, Bloody Dick, and the Bottle Fiend were the kind of people that Deadwood liked to talk about, and the respectable merchants, the Bullocks, Stars, Ayreses, Adamses, Fischels, and

Hunters went about their constructive business unsung and usually unremembered.

Conversely, the antics of some of the upstairs girls often drew tolerant smiles from locals and attention from the press. A newspaper once reported that a working girl named Annie Carr drew a crowd and an arrest for indecent exposure when she danced on the front porch of a club called The 400, "with not enough clothing on to wad a shotgun."

Those same newspapers carried disguised advertisements for the bordellos for many years, alongside sad news reports of young women who had succumbed to overdoses of morphine and laudanum.

Burdened by drunk miners, demanding bosses, low self-esteem, and bartending boyfriends who often left them bruised with black eyes, Deadwood's frontier prostitutes more often dealt with a misery of a decidedly smaller dimension. They came with the setting sun, scurrying through hallways, closets, and snug cribs where ladies of the night were endlessly distracted from entertaining guests until the yellow orb again climbed above the tree line.

That nightly nemesis, numbering perhaps in the thousands, were four-legged, long-tailed, big-bellied rats and a mighty mischief of mice that inundated the Badlands, nesting by day in the darkness beneath the floorboards of ramshackle huts and quickly constructed saloons and brothels, awaiting their ritual nocturnal hunt for food and debris discarded by the hoard of humans who came to inhabit Deadwood Gulch. Their presence, disdained by the wealthy as well as the poor, simply drove the upstairs girls nuts.

That disdain for the dirty, darting, disgusting rodents eventually would lead to an innovative resolution from a generous john who truly felt the plight of the women of the night. It came in the form of one freighter named Phatty Thompson, and some four-legged friends he found wandering around in Cheyenne, Wyoming, according to an account in *Deadwood Magazine*.

One sultry evening in Deadwood's heyday, after a long day on a dusty trail, Phatty was befriending a downtown dancehall girl who suggested that a cat might make her humble home more comfortable. No stranger to upstairs cribs, where vermin often attempted a threesome, Phatty also was well aware that mice traps in the tiny town of Deadwood were at a premium.

Those insights, gleaned from sweaty sessions with several seductresses and close personal observation over time, would lead Phatty to haul what was arguably the most famous load of cargo to ever reach the remote wilderness outpost known as Deadwood. According to some, it also introduced a new word to the English language.

Phatty Thompson drove his team of oxen and empty wagon all the way back to Cheyenne, a treacherous overland haul not to be discounted. When he finally arrived in what would become Wyoming's capital, Phatty rounded up a herd of idle local boys and asked them to assemble a clowder of stray cats as quickly as they could. As an incentive, he reportedly offered the youngsters a goodly sum of 25 cents for every healthy feline they were able to capture and deliver to him.

While the boys were off searching every alleyway and hiding spot, Phatty took his time fashioning crates as cages for his wagon, and awaited his anticipated quarry. When the boys returned, likely with gashes and slashes as evidence of their hunt, Phatty examined the cats, determined if they were in merchantable condition, and paid the youngsters accordingly.

Satisfied with his load of eighty-two caterwauling felines, Phatty set out on his return trip to the Black Hills, ascending the foothills and slowly climbing through the forests of ponderosa pines, undoubtedly serenaded along his winding route by the refrain of his mass of mousers, which probably celebrated every thump in the trail.

Phatty and his load were nearing the end of their 273-mile trek when the unthinkable happened. Just past Hill City and only about ten miles from his intended destination in Deadwood, Phatty was negotiating his team through the waters of Spring Creek when his wagon tipped, spilling his entire consignment of kittens, tabbies, and tomcats. Since the critters are not fond of water, the clowder of cats quickly dispersed.

Fortunately, as he sought to reassemble his payload, Phatty was aided by a group of friendly prospectors who soon had the wagon upright and the cargo reloaded. The happy freighter returned the miners' kindness with a few cats of their own.

When the entrepreneurial freighter finally pulled into Deadwood, and word spread of his unusual haul, Phatty Thompson was richly rewarded. After he quickly set up shop on Main Street, selling straight out of the back of his wagon, a flock of upstairs girls floated down to the dusty thoroughfare and, with the help of merchants, madams, and local homeowners, bought out all of Phatty's four-legged feline stock.

Phatty's foray into bringing a load of cats to Deadwood proved lucrative. The least attractive of his moogies brought $10, while his highly prized Maltese cats commanded $25 each.

The identity of the man responsible for bringing the load of cats to town has long been debated. Some have credited Wild Bill Hickok's friend, Colorado Charlie Utter, with the deed, while the *Black Hills Daily Times* reported on September 3, 1879, that a man named Alexander Davidson transported a load to Deadwood from Denver.

"Regardless of who was responsible, Deadwood's profitable delivery of friendly felines was a big event," writer Dustin Floyd reported in the April 2006 edition of *Deadwood Magazine*. "So big, some locals say, it led to the creation of a new word to describe a brothel: cathouse."

On its face, Floyd said, the concept seemed plausible. After all, the western frontier had spawned a number of new words for the English language, including *cowboy*, *rodeo*, and *lasso*. Even the *Dictionary of American Slang, Third Edition* seemed to support the notion that Deadwood's cat sale could be credited with creating the word, noting that *cathouse* was not in common use until the 1890s. That would have given the word nearly two decades to catch on with the rest of the country, he noted.

"However, the dictionary doesn't have any other good news for this particular legend," Floyd wrote after his scholarly study. "It directly links 'cathouse' with the word 'cat,' which used to carry a secondary definition in the English language that meant 'prostitute'—or any anatomical features she might have employed in her line of work. But how early were felines being equated with the girls of the sex trade?"

According to Floyd and the *Oxford English Dictionary, Second Edition,* very early. The now-obsolete substitution of the word "cat" for "prostitute" was established as early as 1401, when the word appeared in "Friar Daw's Reply," a poem in the Middle English *Piers Plowman* tradition. Although the exact meaning of the word in the poem is debatable, Floyd found the definition had been unquestionably cemented by 1670, when an early dictionary entry for *cat* followed the word with the phrase, "a common whore."

Consequently, while Phatty Thompson's entrepreneurial exploits in bringing the first load of cats to Deadwood to satisfy the cravings of his favorite upstairs girls likely did not generate a new label for houses of prostitution, it certainly did fill his pockets with coins, which he undoubtedly shared freely with his girls well into the night.

Chapter 5

Crazy Horse: Our Strange Man

He was revered by his people and feared by nearly everyone else, including US Cavalry soldiers intent on exterminating the threat on the western plains, and rival tribes competing for the same diminishing quarry on a shrinking range.

Known by three names during his short lifetime—Curly, His Horses Looking, and, finally, Crazy Horse (*Ta-Shunka-Witco*)—to his fellow Oglala Lakota he was "Our Strange Man," a devout loner, fearsome warrior, and charitable friend whose legend has lingered more than a century and a quarter after his untimely demise.

Born on the banks of the rippling waters of Rapid Creek (some say the Belle Fourche River) about 1840, as a young man Crazy Horse witnessed the growing encroachment on Native lands, first from French traders, trappers, and explorers and gradually, like a wave flowing over the grasslands, pioneering white settlers riding wagons and horses and even on foot, all heading west for newfound homes.

Other than a few dates of battles in which Crazy Horse was known to have fought, he remains an obscure figure in western history, primarily because he not only shunned white people invading his lands, he tended to avoid people altogether, preferring an isolated existence.

When Pulitzer Prize–winning author Larry McMurtry, who penned *Lonesome Dove* and *The Last Picture Show*, wrote his short novel titled *Crazy Horse*, he encountered a conundrum, and scant research into the legendary Lakota leader that was filled with speculation. He admitted as much in the lead-in to his second chapter:

> It is as well to say firmly at the outset that any study of Crazy Horse will be, of necessity, an exercise in assumption, conjecture, and surmise. We have more verifiable facts about another young warrior Alexander, called the Great, who lived more than two thousand years earlier than Crazy Horse and whose career is also richly encrusted with legend, than we do about the strange man of the Oglalas.
>
> Crazy Horse lived about three and a half decades as a member of a hunting-raiding-gathering tribe that was not at all date obsessed. The dates and places where the historian can firmly place him are white dates: mainly the dates of a few battles he is known to have taken part in. For most of his life he not only avoided white people, he avoided people, spending many days alone on the prairies, dreaming, drifting, hunting.

Born the son of Crazy Horse, an Oglala holy man, Curly, as he was first known due to his light-colored, curly hair and relatively light complexion, killed a buffalo in his early years and was among the first young men in his *tiospaye* (family) to ride a wild horse. He lost his mother, a member of the Brule tribe, when he was only a youngster.

At an early age, Curly became quite adept at breaking wild horses as well as stealing them from other tribes. Those accomplishments in his early teens gained him wide respect and led his father to cast aside the son's initial moniker and replace it with His Horses Looking. When he was still a teenager, following his bravery in an encounter with Arapaho warriors, his father gave him his own name of Crazy Horse, and the elder shaman thereafter was known as Worm.

As was the case with virtually every young Plains Indian warrior, Crazy Horse set out on a vision quest in 1854, when he was just thirteen or fourteen years of age. In that solitary odyssey and sacred rite of passage, he was said to have wandered on the prairies for four days without food or water, hoping the spirits would provide him with guidance on his path in life. When that vision finally arrived, he purportedly witnessed an unadorned horseman who commanded that he portray himself in the same manner, sans a war bonnet or any accoutrements. Instead, he was directed to wear a single feather, place a small stone behind an ear, sprinkle his horse with dust before a battle, and never take anything for himself.

Just three years later, Crazy Horse found his first love, Black Buffalo Woman. Before he could even court her, she married a warrior named No Water while Crazy Horse was gone from his village on a raid. More than a decade later, Crazy Horse was still determined to make Black Buffalo Woman his own. In 1868 he eloped with her while No Water was absent from his camp. The couple spent just one night together before No Water returned, reunited with his wife, broke Crazy Horse's jaw, and shot him in the nose. Fearing the brief union would cause violence in the two camps, a truce was arranged in which No Water kept his wife and Crazy Horse received a horse from No Water as compensation for his injuries.

Crazy Horse would eventually marry a woman named Black Shawl, who died of tuberculosis, and later a French-Cheyenne woman named Nellie Larrabee.

Although he lived for extended periods with those wives and among his people, Crazy Horse was said to have rejected many of the norms of Lakota society and preferred his own company, often hunting alone on the prairies.

"There was something of the hermit, the eremite, in him; he was known to walk through his own camp without appearing to notice anybody," McMurtry wrote. "When, late in life, his family began to worry about his tendency to wander off alone in dangerous country, he told them not to worry, there were plenty of caves and holes he could live in; and had it not been for his sense of responsibility to the people of his village—who knew that he would do his best to feed them he might well have slipped away and lived in those caves and holes."

While many writers and historians have spent hundreds of pages putting words in the mouth of Crazy Horse, he was known to have been a man of few words. More importantly, due to his innate desire to be alone, quietly hunting or spending an evening at his campfire, with the exception of a few battles and his murder, the vast majority of Crazy Horse's life went unwitnessed by anyone.

"All this is not to say that we know nothing of Crazy Horse," McMurtry penned. "He was a man, not a myth, and we do know certain things about him. We know enough from the testimony of his close associates to have some idea of the main events of his life, particularly his losses: of his brother, Little Hawk, of his daughter They-Are-Afraid-of-Her, of his friends Hump and Lone Bear, and of Black Buffalo Woman, the love of his life, who married another man. We also know something of his behavior in two or three crucial battles."

Even before the birth of Crazy Horse, whites were moving along the Oregon Trail "like rising flood waters," sparking scattered confrontations between Native Americans and the new settlers and, eventually, signaling the end of a way of life for the Plains Indians who had called the vast American West their home for centuries.

When gold was discovered along the Bozeman Trail in Montana in 1866, the wave of prospectors seeking riches led to renewed clashes, prompting the federal government under General William Tecumseh Sherman to begin building a series of forts in the heart of Sioux territory.

Just four days before Christmas that same year, Crazy Horse found himself in the company of a confederation of Lakota, Arapahoe, and Cheyenne Indian warriors near one of those garrisons called Fort Phil Kearny in eastern Wyoming.

In her poetic and clearly embellished 1942 biography titled *Crazy Horse: The Strange Man of the Oglalas*, Mari Sandoz described the months-long harassment of the fort by Crazy Horse and his compatriots and the final confrontation in which Crazy Horse acted as a decoy to lure eighty white soldiers from the fort into an ambush. The bloody conclusion came to be known variously as the Battle of the Hundred-in-the-Hands and the Fetterman Massacre.

> Now the troops began to back up the steep icy ridge, fighting as they withdrew, some riding and turning to shoot, some leading their horses and firing from a knee behind them. They kept in a close little bunch half lost in the smoke of their guns and the warriors couldn't get among them. Once when they pushed the whites too hard, one brave soldier dropped back to protect the rest, yelling names at the Indians, firing with pistol and gun as fast as he could reload until a Minneconjou rode up and shot an arrow through his breast. In the middle of that fighting the warrior stopped to take the scalp, for this white man had been very brave....
>
> Then the last white man was down and only a dog was left to run from among the rocks. He started away along the trail towards the fort, looking back several times and going on. Crazy Horse watched him, wondering that none among them had seen him until the whites were all scattered on the ground.

When the last shot had been fired on that frigid winter night, eighty soldiers had died. Anything of value, including coats, pants, boots, rings, watches, and firearms, was quickly stripped from the dead bodies, which were as quickly mangled as a message to General Sherman. Then the warriors gathered up their wounded and thirteen dead and abandoned the scene as more soldiers exited the fort.

When Crazy Horse and his band of warriors attacked another small fort in 1867, the message was finally heard and Sherman visited the region, meeting with tribal leaders to seek peace, which resulted in the 1868 Fort Laramie Treaty that ceded all of the lands west of the Missouri River to the Big Horn Mountains to the Sioux as long as the sun shone and the rivers ran. But the respite would be brief.

Crazy Horse sat out the treaty talks, a lifelong practice, instead preferring to harass soldiers and settlers, and conduct raids on trading posts and enemy tribes.

Over the next four years, Crazy Horse continued raiding his enemies. By 1872, with railroads extending west and tensions rising between the tribes, the ever-present settlers, and the US Army, Crazy Horse had joined Sitting Bull. Together they conducted a raid on four hundred soldiers in which the horse Crazy Horse was riding was shot out from beneath him as he made a rash dash toward the enemy troops.

The following year, after Lieutenant Colonel George Armstrong Custer and his 7th Cavalry crossed into Indian territory along the Yellowstone River, Crazy Horse likely caught his first glimpse of "Yellow Hair." When Crazy Horse and his band of renegades caught the soldiers napping, they attempted to steal their horses, but were repelled after a brief skirmish. In 1874, Custer would lead an expedition into the Black Hills in violation of the

Fort Laramie Treaty and, when his men discovered gold along the banks of French Creek and the find was announced in eastern newspapers, it set off a stampede of prospectors all headed for the Hills.

With their lands being violated by miners, muleskinners, and madams, in 1876 Crazy Horse, Sitting Bull, and a large contingent of tribes were peacefully camped along the Little Big Horn River in southeastern Montana Territory. In early June, General George Crook, who had recently raided a village he incorrectly believed to be that of Crazy Horse, was on the warpath against the Lakota and Cheyenne for failing to adhere to an ultimatum demanding they return to their reservations in Dakota Territory and Nebraska.

Crook and his 1,050 troops, augmented by 260 Shoshone and Crow scouts, had ridden into Montana's Rosebud Valley where his scouts spotted the encampment. Crazy Horse commanded a force of warriors nearly equal to that of Crook and on June 17, he attacked Crook's forces in a pitched battle that lasted six hours. While neither side could claim victory, Crook inevitably did, even though Crazy Horse and his band of Lakota and Cheyenne had elected to disengage at the Battle of the Rosebud. When the dust settled, Crook had lost ten soldiers and had twenty-one wounded, similar to Native American casualties. More importantly, the skirmish had rendered one of Crook's three columns useless and it was effectively eliminated from the campaign for the following two months.

McMurtry lamented the aftermath of the battle, the role Crook's Native scouts had likely played in preventing his defeat and potential embarrassment, and noted widely different casualty counts, depending on who was doing the reporting:

> Because the Indians left the field when the day was over, Crook claimed a victory, but nobody believed him, including (probably) himself. . . . Neither side could mount a fully decisive offensive, and both sides suffered unusually high casualties but kept fighting. . . . The body count for the two sides varies with the commentator: George Hyde puts Crook's loss as high as fifty-seven men, a number that presumably includes many Crows and Shoshones who fell that day; Stephen Ambrose says it was twenty-eight men; Stanley Vestal says it was ten; and Robert Utley and Evan S. Connell Jr. claim it was nine. The attacking Sioux and Cheyennes may themselves have lost over thirty men, an enormous casualty rate for a native force. Accustomed as we are to the wholesale slaughter of the two world wars, or even of the Civil War, it is hard to keep in mind that when Indian fought Indian a death count of more than three or four was unusual.

Some historians have contended that the Battle of the Rosebud, while considered a stalemate, led to the disaster that would befall the US Army eight days later because Crook had failed to rout the Indian warriors or even give chase, boosting their morale with deadly consequences.

Enter George Armstrong Custer and his 7th Cavalry, whom he claimed could fight through the entire Sioux nation in an afternoon, and live to tell about it. Of course, he didn't. In fact, when he and his men finally reached the battleground along the banks of the Greasy Grass after marching most of the night, they were exhausted and in no condition to fight as many as two thousand warriors who had amassed along the Little Big Horn.

While his fellow Lakota and Cheyenne were attending to business on the morning of the battle, Crazy Horse used red pigment to mark a bloody hand on each of his horse's hips and reportedly drew an arrow and a bloody red hand on both sides of the animal's neck. It was June 25, 1876, a day that would mark one of the most epic battles in history.

Alerted by scouts to the presence of advancing troops well before the first shot was fired, the tribesmen were ready and eager for a fight, even while finding it incomprehensible that anyone, even the US Army, would take on such a formidable force. But when they did, Crazy Horse, perhaps in command of as many as one thousand warriors himself, seized the high ground and prevented Custer from establishing a defensive position. When it was all over, Custer was dead, shot through the breast and the temple, as were the nine officers and the 280 enlisted men who had followed him into his disastrous battle.

In the following days, the entire Native American encampment packed up and scattered on the plains. Sitting Bull and his band fled to Canada, while Crazy Horse and his followers returned to the Black Hills, camping near Bear Butte near present-day Sturgis, while raiding miners and wagons at will through that fall.

That winter, Crazy Horse and his nine hundred followers suffered through frigid weather and brutal conditions. By May, the

Strange Man realized that he might be able to remain free by hiding out in the Hills, but his people would be far worse for the decision. So, with his ragtag band in tow, as well as two thousand horses, he traveled to the Red Cloud Agency at Fort Robinson in northwestern Nebraska and, for the first time in his life, gave up his gun and sat down in council with white men.

General Crook soon arrived, taking credit for the "surrender" of Crazy Horse. He promised the now legendary Lakota leader, but never a chief, his own agency in a place of his choosing, and said he would allow his people to leave the agency for forty-day buffalo hunts. But those promises were never fulfilled, and Crazy Horse soon developed a disdain for life at Fort Robinson with its idleness, boredom, and petty jealousies.

McMurtry, Sandoz, and other authors have addressed two occurrences that ultimately led to the death of Crazy Horse. In council with his captors, translator, scout, and Crazy Horse's friend Frank Grouard reportedly told the white soldiers that Crazy Horse intended to fight to his death and kill every white man he encountered. Others who understood Sioux were astounded and attempted to correct the mistranslation. Whether they were successful has never been determined. Then in September 1877, when General Crook had returned to Fort Robinson for further talks with Crazy Horse, an Indian woman named Women's Dress approached him and claimed Crazy Horse would shake his hand, then plunge a knife into him.

Concerned, Crook ordered Crazy Horse taken into custody, but when tribal police and soldiers arrived at Crazy Horse's camp to arrest him, they learned he had made an unannounced trip to the

Spotted Tail Agency some forty miles away. Escorted back to Fort Robinson and told he would meet the fort's commander for discussions, Crazy Horse was instead led past the general's office and toward the fort's guardhouse. It was near midnight on September 6, 1877.

When Crazy Horse sensed what was happening, he whirled around on his escorts and a struggle ensued. Crazy Horse brandished a knife cloaked under a blanket and cut Little Big Man, a tribal policeman. As guns were locked and loaded and pointed in the direction of Crazy Horse, a white private named William Gentles advanced and plunged his bayonet into the kidneys of Crazy Horse. The proud Lakota who yearned for a vanishing life, slipped to the floor, mortally wounded, and died. His body was secreted away from the scene by his fellow Lakota and buried in an unknown location along the banks of Wounded Knee Creek.

Despite his violent death, the legend of Crazy Horse lives on today, emerging from stone in the Black Hills he so loved. When completed, Crazy Horse Memorial, a tribute to all Native Americans, will be the largest work of art on earth, eclipsing even nearby Mount Rushmore National Memorial.

The fitting monumental tribute was begun in 1948 by famed sculptor Korczak Ziolkowski after he was asked by Chief Henry Standing Bear to carve a Native American monument, saying, "My fellow chiefs and I would like the white man to know that the red man has great heroes also."

Ziolkowski and his wife, Ruth, would spend the remaining years of their lives creating a Native American monument on

This photograph shows the model for Crazy Horse Memorial in the foreground and the actual mountain carving in progress in the background.

Thunderhead Mountain. Today, that work is carried on by their children and supported by more than one million annual visitors.

CHAPTER 6

The Thoen Stone—Fact or Fraud?

Although French fur traders undoubtedly passed through the Black Hills far earlier than other explorers or prospectors, the first evidence of visitors of European descent came with the fabled 1874 Custer Expedition. But a certain stone may contradict that legend.

Backed by one thousand soldiers and one hundred wagons laden with supplies, Colonel George Armstrong Custer led his men from Fort Abraham Lincoln near present-day Bismarck on a two-month odyssey, beginning July 2, 1874, and ending the following August 29.

It was, as Ernest Grafe and Paul Horsted described in their meticulously detailed account, *Exploring with Custer: The 1874 Black Hills Expedition*, a journey to the last unknown place. In fact, until that time, due to the 1868 Fort Laramie Treaty between the Lakota and the federal government, which had ceded everything between the Missouri River and the Big Horn Mountains to the tribe, it remained a vast tract of uncharted territory.

Custer and his troops set out ostensibly as a military expedition intended to map the million-acre wilderness. With Custer's cadre of miners, newspaper correspondents, and a lone photographer named William Illingworth, as well as at least fifteen soldiers who kept detailed diaries, the expedition became one of the most well-documented military exercises ever conducted in the American West.

When Custer's men confirmed the presence of gold midway through their journey along a stretch of stream near what would become Custer City, the news set off a flood of fortune-seekers, all hell-bent on filling their gold pans and pokes with a pinch of color that would set them up for life. That search for a prosperous tomorrow would lead many prospectors northward, where the motherlode was soon discovered in a gold-filled gulch known as Deadwood. And the rest, as they say, is history.

But, was Custer's corps really the first to find gold in the Black Hills? A simple stone slab, since the subject of much doubt and abundant conjecture, would argue otherwise.

On March 14, 1887, just eleven years after a throng of ten thousand miners, merchants, and muleskinners had descended on Deadwood Gulch, Louis Thoen and his younger brother, Ivan, were working in a rock quarry on Lookout Mountain, on the eastern flank of the new settlement of Spearfish. The pair were searching for sandstone, from which many of the buildings in Spearfish would be constructed. In the process, Louis unearthed a flat-sided piece of sandstone, measuring about ten by eight by two-and-a-half inches.

The discovery of a sandstone slab, in itself, was nothing to raise a ruckus. But the words crudely carved in either face of the block of rock would test the mettle of any historian, challenge the claim that Custer and his men had been the first whites to explore the Hills, and lead to a lingering debate over the Thoen Stone's authenticity that has continued ever since the day Louis Thoen lifted that chunk of sandstone from the ground.

When Louis found the piece half buried in dirt, he could read a portion of its inscription, which said, "Indians hunting me." Intrigued by the discovery, he took the slab home in hopes of deciphering the entirety of its message. Once he had carefully removed the remaining dirt stuck to the block of sandstone, he found the following missive etched into its face: "Came to these hills in 1833 seven of us, De Lacompt, Ezra Kind, G.W. Wood, T. Brown, R. Kent, Wm. King, Indian Crow all ded but me Ezra Kind, killed by Ind beyond the high hill got our gold June 1834."

On the opposite side, the slab was inscribed: "Got all the gold we could carry our ponys all got by the Indians I hav lost my gun and nothing to eat and Indians hunting me."

Although skeptics have ever since questioned the validity of the Thoen Stone, its authenticity would mean that gold seekers had entered the Black Hills forty-one years before Custer and his men ever set foot in the sacred land of the Sioux, forty years before its official settlement, and more than three decades before the Fort Laramie Treaty had ever been contemplated, let alone signed.

Ever since the discovery of the Thoen Stone, as it came to be called, historians and amateur investigators have sought to determine its legitimacy and determine whether a ragtag band of

THE THOEN STONE—FACT OR FRAUD?

Courtesy Deadwood History Inc., Adams Museum Collection

Historians and amateur sleuths have debated the authenticity of the Thoen Stone ever since brothers Louis and Ivan Thoen uncovered it near Spearfish, South Dakota, in March 1887. The unusual artifact remains on permanent display at the Adams Museum in Deadwood.

frontier fortune-seekers had indeed explored the Black Hills in search of gold long before it has been commonly acknowledged. And several have made their case, tracking the seven men listed on the slab.

Frank Thomson spent nearly fourteen years tracing the party's men before writing *The Thoen Stone: A Saga of the Black Hills*. In his work, Thomson sought to determine whether those listed on the stone tablet had actually existed, or whether the whole enterprise was a sick hoax perpetrated by some bored stonemason. In the end,

Thomson concluded that every word written on the Thoen Stone was the undeniable truth.

In his extensive research, the author discovered that a group of men left Independence, Missouri, in the spring of 1833, intent on finding a route to Santa Fe, New Mexico. Along the way, Thomson surmised, the group befriended a member of the Crow Tribe who told them of rich veins of gold to be found in the Black Hills, which quickly led the entourage to change their travel plans.

Thomson claimed to have traced the majority of the men to their modern-day descendants, who confirmed they had ancestors who had disappeared after heading west in 1833, never to be heard from again. Kent's surviving family members even reported that their forefathers had told stories of receiving letters from him in the 1830s that stated he had acquired all the gold he could possibly desire and would be returning home soon.

In an exceptionally researched 2013 story for the *Sidney Sun-Telegraph*, award-winning Nebraska columnist M. Timothy Nolting took Thomson's study a step further, delving into the origins of each of the men in Ezra Kind's group, tracing their family history and confirming that they had banded together in a quest for gold in the Black Hills long before Custer's expedition rolled into the region. And, according to the writer, they left other evidence behind in addition to the Thoen Stone. Nolting wrote:

> They discovered that gold in the Black Hills near present day Spearfish, South Dakota beyond "the high hill" of Crow Peak on Spotted Tail Gulch. During the Black Hills gold rush of 1876–77 placer miners dug for gold on

Spotted Tail Creek and found the remains of an old cabin. Nothing was left of the cabin except for a few of the base logs and at the center of the foundation grew pine trees as much as nine inches in diameter and many feet high. Could this have been the cabin of the seven? Also, near the site, miners dug shafts to bedrock and found, thirteen feet below the surface, a rusted shovel and pick. These items, so far beneath the surface were certain signs of active mining many years, perhaps decades, before.

Even more remarkable, Nolting reported that he was able to confirm not only the existence of all but one of the party, but that they had traveled together.

Of the seven men, five have been reasonably traced to families that had relatives who went off in search of gold and never returned. Family members tell of a relative Wm. King who went west with a gentleman named Kent. T. Brown and Indian Crow left from the same North Carolina community to go west and were never heard from again. R. Kent and Ezra Kind also left family to seek their fortunes and left behind notes claiming to have found all the gold they could want, but never returned home.

"Only G. W. Wood remains a mystery," Nolting concluded.

For decades since its discovery, historians and amateur sleuths have debated the authenticity of the Thoen Stone. Some, including researchers and writers Thomson and Nolting, wrote that they had little doubt the men had entered the Black Hills more than four decades before Custer, found gold, and lost their lives because of it.

Others, including locals and skeptical scholars, questioned its legitimacy, noting it was curious that Louis Thoen, an experienced stonemason, just happened to stumble upon a slab of sandstone with script legible enough to decipher after fifty-four years of exposure to sun, wind, rain, and winter snows.

Regardless of its authenticity, the Thoen Stone continues to captivate thousands of Black Hills visitors each year. The sandstone specimen was loaned to Deadwood's Adams Museum in the 1930s by Louis Thoen's daughters, who sought a permanent and secure home for the unusual artifact. Ultimately, the women willed it to the museum in 1965, where it has remained on display ever since as a vital part of the institution's permanent collection.

Chapter 7

Lame Johnny and the Lost Gold

Legends of lost gold, sometimes stashed by fugitive outlaws with a posse closing in, are as old as the Wild West.

Whether the loot came from a stagecoach, a bank, unfortunate travelers, a railroad train, or a treasure coach transporting precious metals from a remote mine, the lure of ill-gotten gains was simply too much for too many who preferred to rob others of the fruits of their labors, rather than working and finding their own fortune.

Historians have long lamented the rough and often deadly environment that accompanied the last great gold rush in the Black Hills in the 1870s. Once renegade Indians were tamed or returned to reservations by the late 1870s, law-abiding folks only had outlaws, highwaymen, and bandits to contend with.

Author Watson Parker, whose wonderful book *Deadwood: The Golden Years* recounts the town's earliest period in vivid detail, noted there were sixteen murders in Lawrence County in 1878. Newspapers in Cheyenne, Wyoming, suggested the name of the gold-filled gulch be changed from "Deadwood" to "Deadman," and others claimed that cemeteries ranked among the most thriving businesses.

Meanwhile commercial clubs promoting the region claimed newcomers "would be as secure here as they would be in any part of the East." But Parker, always captivated by first-person accounts, quoted a visitor from Manitowoc, Wisconsin, who seemed to have a contrary view, albeit laced with a hint of exaggeration.

> Every man in Deadwood carries about fourteen pounds of firearms hitched in his belt, and they never pass any words. The fellow that gets his gun out first is best man, and they lug off the other fellow's body. Our graveyard is a big institution, and a growing one. Sometimes, however, the place is right quiet. I've know[n] times when a man wasn't killed for twenty-four hours. Then, again, perhaps, they'll lay out five or six a day. When a man gets too handy with his shootin' irons, and kills five or six, they'll think he isn't safe, and somebody pops him over to rid the place of him. They don't kill him for what he has done, but for what he's liable to do. I suppose the average deaths amount to about one hundred a month.

Those types of lurid accounts of life in the Old West, carried by newspapers throughout the United States and around the globe, struck a chord with many would-be adventurers seeking an escape from their daily drudgery and ceaseless toil in America's crowded urban areas and quiet farms. But in his early years, there was little evidence that Cornelius Donahue would join the procession of men headed west, nor was it likely he would become a notorious outlaw and eventually become a wanted man.

Born sometime around 1854 in Philadelphia, then a bustling metropolis of one hundred twenty-one thousand residents and the fourth largest city in the United States, Donahue was apparently orphaned at a young age, or was simply abandoned by his destitute parents. In his youth, Donahue studied for a decade at Girard College, a center for elementary through high school students that took in impoverished and orphaned boys. School records list his birthdate as October 6, 1854, and indicate he was well behaved and excelled in academics.

Enrolled in 1862, in the midst of the Civil War, Donahue would endure his scholastic studies at Girard until 1872, when the call of the wild reached his ears and sent him scurrying south for the rangelands of Texas.

In short order, while learning the ropes as a hired hand on various ranches, Donahue was snared by the smart talk of the wrong herd of cowboys. And, they inevitably saddled him with some bad habits. Bands of Apache raiders frequently visited the remote ranch, stealing entire herds of horses under the cloak of darkness. Coached by his fellow cowhands, Donahue quickly became adept at helping his compadres pinch the ponies right back, as well as a few other horses that did not happen to belong to the ranch.

With a distinctive limp some have attributed to a bout of polio in his youth, Cornelius Donahue likely stood out from his fellow ranch hands—and no self-respecting cowboy in the Lone Star State would have wanted to be known as "Cornelius." Therefore, as the band's horse-borrowing business grew more daring, Donahue adopted the alias John Hurley, a moniker that his friends quickly distorted to "Lame Johnny."

As their brazen pilfering of ponies continued, the horse thefts eventually drew the attention of Texas marshals, who began tracking the gang in the 1870s. As the law was closing in on Lame Johnny and his badly bathed associates, news filtered down from the newspapers to the saloon patrons of a great gold strike in the Black Hills of Dakota Territory. By that fabled summer of 1876, Lame Johnny was likely considering a noose around his neck if he stayed in Texas too long, or the prospect of promised riches over the horizon to the north if he vanished. It did not take him long to choose an option.

On a spring day in 1876, Cheyenne freighter John Murphy was preparing to take another load of supplies to Deadwood when he was approached by a mild-mannered man with a noticeable limp who called himself John A. Hurley. The young man inquired about working his way to Deadwood with the freighting outfit and, always in need of help on the dusty, dangerous trail, Murphy readily agreed and found a horse for Hurley.

Lame Johnny arrived in the Black Hills to the sounds of commerce and myriad gold camps just learning to stand on their own. With sawmills cranking and hammers pounding, ramshackle towns including Custer City, Deadwood, Lead, and Hill City were rising from the forest floor, perched beside gurgling brooks and nestled in the shadows of towering granite peaks.

Breathing in the clear mountain air and the smell of money from the gold mines, Lame Johnny sincerely sought a fresh start and an alternative to looking over his shoulder in fear of a pursing sheriff. Initially, he tried his hand at prospecting, but most of the best spots had already been claimed. Besides, he quickly learned that standing knee-deep in a frigid stream, particularly with a bum leg, was a tough way to make a living.

In addition, early-day Black Hills miners were not particularly friendly, a condition brought on by a general suspicion of others and the fact that nearly everybody was well armed and disposed to drinking whiskey. One day, while Lame Johnny was panning for gold in Castle Creek, a band of Lakota natives reportedly stole his horses. As an experienced horse-thief, Johnny would have none of that.

Historical accounts contend Lame Johnny found another horse and rode to the Red Cloud Agency where he murdered a guard and unleased three hundred horses that stampeded for the Black Hills. That same scenario would play out several times that summer of '76 and, by the end of it, Lame Johnny had decided that the prospects of prospecting were not nearly as good as he initially imagined.

He spent a stint as a deputy sheriff in Custer County, but soon lost interest in protecting other people for meager pay and long hours.

Fortunately, Donahue had taken something away from his time at Girard College: a decade of schooling that set him above many of those vying for cushy desk jobs at the major mining operations. And the granddaddy on the block of rock known as the Black Hills was the Homestake Gold Mine at Lead.

The Homestake, which would eventually operate for 125 years, tunnel a mile-and-a-half underground, and generate as much as $1.2 billion in gold, had been purchased by publishing magnate George Hearst in 1876, for the then-astonishing sum of $200,000. By the conclusion of 1887, the Homestake had already generated $3,843,750 in dividends.

And, Cornelius "Lame Johnny" Donahue, who likely didn't want to be anywhere near his earlier alias tied to horse-thieving, got in on Homestake's growing ground floor. Armed with his schooling rather than a six-gun, Lame Johnny limped into Homestake's offices in Lead and landed a job as a bookkeeper.

Relatively educated and seemingly upstanding, albeit aided by a high-heel in one boot to offset his deformed foot, Donahue spent months acquainting himself with Homestake's frequent shipments of gold bullion to Cheyenne, Wyoming, Denver, Colorado, and other far-flung centers of commerce.

After a series of attempted robberies of stagecoaches carrying Homestake gold, some successful and others not, Donahue also was possibly privy to security measures the mining company instituted to thwart the thieves. Chief among these were two steel-plated "treasure coaches" constructed by the Cheyenne and Black Hills Stage Company, one labeled Slaughter and the other named for the Civil War ironclad USS *Monitor*.

Horse-drawn and wooden-wheeled, the coaches were an engineering marvel, lined with steel plates five-sixteenth of an inch thick, a strongbox that manufacturers claimed would take at least a day (others say six days) to open without aid of the combination, and portals in each door, allowing guards to fire at any threat.

While those details were not immediately on the mind of Donahue as he performed his daily bookkeeping duties at

Homestake Gold Mine's *Monitor* was an ironclad fortress on wheels, used to transport gold bullion and dust from its mine in Lead, South Dakota, to commercial centers in Cheyenne, Wyoming, and Denver. Cornelius "Lame Johnny" Donahue and his gang were suspected of robbing the treasure coach in September 1878.

Courtesy Deadwood History Inc., Homestake Mining Company Collection, @Flickr

Homestake's general offices, they would come in handy at a later date. For Cornelius Donahue was not one to stay focused, or employed, for too long.

After nearly two years of living and working in the Black Hills, Cornelius Donahue thought he had outrun his past in a distant place where no one knew his face. But on one day of reckoning, all that would change when someone recognized him as Lame Johnny, a wanted man who had fled Texas a few steps ahead of the law. In a matter of hours, he had vacated his job at Homestake. In a matter of days, he had returned to his former life, stealing horses and rustling cattle. It wasn't long before Lame Johnny and his ragtag group of loners, losers, and lost souls stepped up their game to include stage robbery.

"Hardly an early issue of the Deadwood newspapers is without its news of 'midnight assaults of a band of coach-robbing ruffians,'" historian Parker observed. "The bulk of the bandits' activities took place in the southern end of the Hills, for too many well-armed and ill-tempered miners worked and roamed around Deadwood for a highwayman in that area to feel secure in his profession."

That didn't stop the Pennsylvanian-turned-cowboy-turned-outlaw. For months, Lame Johnny's gang terrorized the stage routes, robbing coaches, pilfering anything of value from passengers, and living off the fruits of the labors of others. When pursued by a posse, the outlaws would simply vanish into the ponderosa pine forests and creek-carved canyons of the Black Hills. But after a succession of robberies, and a slew of descriptions that included a man with a limp, lawmen began to pursue Lame Johnny with some vigor.

Always on the move, forever in hiding, with that keen sense arising again that he should keep an eye over his shoulder lest he be pistol-whipped or worse, shot by a zealous marshal, Lame Johnny began to consider his future. He certainly recalled the weekly routes taken by Homestake's treasure coaches, and he finally decided they represented an opportunity for a one-time, last-ditch "big score" that could set him up and get him gone from this place where the walls and the law were quickly closing in.

With his working knowledge of Homestake security measures, Lame Johnny knew that which he coveted would be transported in the Monitor, the ironclad fort and arsenal on wheels, with heavily armed guards in tow. Furthermore, he also recognized that Homestake favored shipping most of its gold in two-hundred-pound ingots, a practice intended to discourage robbers, as one gold bar could prove more than a packhorse could carry.

On the morning of September 26, 1878, Lame Johnny and his band of outlaws rode into Canyon Springs Station some thirty-seven miles southwest of Deadwood in eastern Wyoming about the same time the Monitor was departing Lead with its load of gold, a driver, three guards, and two passengers, all of whom wished to arrive in Cheyenne without incident. The bandits secured the station, locked attendant William Miner in a grain room, ducked into the barn, and awaited their intended target.

When the treasure coach finally pulled into Canyon Springs Station to change a team of horses and take a brief rest, there was no one there to greet them. Driver Gene Barnett and guard Gale Hill had just climbed down from the stagecoach when the first shots were fired. Passenger Hugh Campbell died in the first volley, while Hill was seriously wounded.

As the two sides continued facing off in a fierce firefight, shotgun messenger Scott Davis positioned himself inside the coach, fired through the porthole, and killed one of the gang-members named "Big Nose" McLaughlin and reportedly wounded another. After Davis finally exited the wagon, Lame Johnny and his two remaining men commandeered the coach and rode off into the woods in an easterly direction.

Despite the manufacturer's statements to the contrary, the safe did not prove impregnable. In fact, Lame Johnny and his remaining gang members had little trouble opening it. And when they did, they found they had struck the motherlode.

Inside the safe, they discovered hundreds of dollars' worth of jewelry, $500 in diamonds, $3,500 in currency, and seven hundred pounds of gold dust, nuggets, and bullion. Shortly after the heist, Homestake estimated the total loss at about $140,000. But in today's dollars, the gold alone would be worth more than $13 million.

The highwaymen loaded their loot in a two-wheeled wagon and stole away through steep-sided canyons and along flowing streambeds to their preferred hideout near Buffalo Gap, located on the southeastern flank of the Black Hills.

When the treasure coach had not arrived at its next scheduled stop, the Jenney Stockade to the south, three stage guards set out to find out what had happened. The guards, a famed bounty hunter named Boone May, Bill Sample, and Jesse Brown, soon stumbled on surviving stagecoach messenger Scott Davis, who had acquired a horse from a neighboring ranch. When they finally reached Canyon Springs Station, scene of the robbery, they discovered an abandoned treasure coach, its secure vault empty, the station manager subdued in the granary, and other stage employees gagged and tied to trees in the neighboring woods.

News of the daring and deadly assault and robbery quickly spread throughout the region and, when Homestake posted a sizeable reward, lawmen, vigilantes, and a string of wide-eyed posses searched every hideout and pursued every lead.

One month after the brazen holdup, Homestake and the stage line reported that more than half the loot had already been recovered. But Lame Johnny remained at large and his getaway wagon and two large gold bars had yet to be found.

Early on in the investigation, Lame Johnny's pronounced limp had earned him a top spot on the list of suspects sought in

This 1889 photograph shows part of the Homestake works in Lead, South Dakota. After providing employment to Lame Johnny for two years, Homestake became his target for a multimillion-dollar gold heist.

connection with the holdup, and well-known livestock detective Frank "Whispering" Smith remained in pursuit.

That fall, when Lame Johnny ventured to the Pine Ridge Indian Reservation to acquire ponies in his customary fashion, he and Smith would finally connect when the lawman recognized his quarry, arrested him, then transported Lame Johnny to a jail in nearby Chadron, Nebraska.

In the ensuing weeks, Smith and his associates would take extraordinary measures to ensure that Lame Johnny would remain in custody as they returned him to Deadwood to stand trial. A blacksmith was hired to fashion leg irons for Lame Johnny, which were then riveted to a metal plate fastened to the floor of the stagecoach.

Shackled, handcuffed, and escorted by Whispering Smith, Jesse Brown, and Boone May, who some historians have argued may have been a man with worse character than those he hunted, Lame Johnny was finally secured in a stagecoach and started his final journey toward justice. But he would never see a courtroom.

As the stagecoach rambled its way up a dusty trail eight miles north of Buffalo Gap, they were stopped by a group of masked men who prevented them from advancing. Suspecting that Lame Johnny was being rescued by surviving members of his gang, and knowing they had no reservations about gunning down guards, Smith and his men didn't put up any fight. Resigned to the loss of their prisoner, the lawmen and their stagecoach were sent on their way.

It didn't take the vigilantes long to pry up the metal plate securing Lame Johnny to the floor of the stagecoach and drag him into the open. When Lame Johnny wouldn't reveal the whereabouts of his hidden gold, it took even less time for his captors to shoot him and drag his bleeding body to the nearest elm tree, tie a rope around his neck, and pull him off the ground.

The next morning, drovers with Pete Oslund's bull train were transporting freight up the same trail when they found Lame Johnny's dead body swinging in the wind. They cut him down and buried his body beneath the elm tree and beside a small creek that would eventually carry his name. Thus ended the short but eventful life of an educated eastern boy turned western horse and cattle thief, as well as the purported instigator of one of the most notorious stagecoach robberies in the Wild West.

But the story of Cornelius "Lame Johnny" Donahue didn't end with his death. Curious local residents reportedly later dug up his gravesite and found his corpse still shackled, but lacking its head. They removed the shackles as well as Lame Johnny's boots and displayed them in local museums and a Buffalo Gap store.

Before it faded away after years of sun, wind, rain, and snow, an epitaph posted on a wooden board above Lame Johnny's grave stated:

Pilgrim Pause!
You're standing on the molding clay of Limping John.
Tread lightly, stranger, on this sod.
For if he moves, you're robbed, by God.

Lame Johnny and several others in his gang went to early graves without ever revealing the fate of the four hundred pounds of gold bullion that remained lost after being secreted away from the Monitor stage—a cache worth more than $7.5 million in today's dollars. But that legend of lost gold still captivates historians and treasure seekers alike, for it may remain undiscovered in its hiding place in the vast wilderness of the Black Hills.

CHAPTER 8

Chief Two Sticks's Departure

It took a long time for the law to reach the vast western frontier of the United States. Due to the Fort Laramie Treaty of 1868, which ceded everything between the Missouri River and the Big Horn Mountains to the Lakota Sioux, it took far longer for the long arm of the law to reach the western fringes of Dakota Territory.

The original territory encompassed most of present-day Wyoming and the Dakotas from 1864 to 1868. From 1868 to 1889, today's North and South Dakota were known simply as Dakota Territory. The territorial capital was initially established in 1861 in Yankton, but was moved to Bismarck in 1883.

North and South Dakota were incorporated into the Union on November 2, 1889, although controversy over which state would be admitted first led President Benjamin Harrison to shuffle the bills and then sign one at random, with the official order going unrecorded.

Nevertheless, while the established townships and farmlands of eastern South Dakota established law enforcement agencies and court systems relatively early, it wasn't until General George Armstrong Custer's 1874 Black Hills Expedition that white men legally stepped foot in the region west of the Missouri River.

Custer's confirmation of gold in abundant quantities in the Black Hills set off a flood of would-be prospectors in search of riches. In their wake came gold camps-turned-towns, churches, commerce, local governments, and, eventually, the law.

Certainly, before the law arrived, and even after, vigilantes meted out justice in their own peculiar way, generally with a long rope tied to a tree or at the end of a smoking six-gun. Even some of the US marshals and bounty hunters of Dakota Territory's earliest days carried in their saddlebags reputations as nasty as those they pursued.

But when the law finally arrived, it did not present drastic changes in daily life for most law-abiding residents of the frontier. They simply went about their work, tending to farmsteads, herding cattle, raising families, and attending small churches on Sundays.

Only the miscreants—those who would rather rob than work and steal than toil—found their pursuits crippled by lawmen appointed to watch out for the civic-minded citizens who sought a new life in the American West.

And, despite dime store novels' assertions to the contrary, early days in western Dakota Territory were relatively peaceful. Certainly, there were stagecoach holdups, a smattering of murders, and a scant number of bank robberies, but, by and large, the need to hang criminals for misdeeds was uncommon.

In fact, between 1876 and 2018, according to the state's Cultural Heritage Center, only nineteen people were executed in western Dakota Territory and the state of South Dakota.

The first to gain that unfortunate retribution was "Crooked Nose" Jack McCall, the no-account drifter who shot James Butler "Wild Bill" Hickok in August 1876 in Deadwood. Although he had initially been found not guilty by a hastily assembled miners' court in the gold camp, he was arrested by a federal marshal in Cheyenne, Wyoming, after bragging about his gunplay in a saloon. The marshal transported McCall to the territorial capital of Yankton, where he was again tried, found guilty, and summarily hanged on March 1, 1877, his body buried in an unmarked grave with the noose still around his neck.

Thomas Egan was hanged in Sioux Falls five years later for the murder of his wife. It took executioners three attempts before they got it right. Decades later, the world learned that Egan had been innocent when his stepdaughter admitted to the crime while on her deathbed.

That same year, 1882, Brave Heart was hanged at Yankton for the murder of a pioneer settler in Sully County in 1879, and James Gilmore was hanged at Deadwood for killing a man on the old Fort Pierre to Deadwood trail. Another decade would pass before James Leehman was hanged for the murder of James H. Burns, and in October 1893, Nathaniel Thompson was hanged at DeSmet for killing his wife's friend. Two months later, Jay Hicks was hanged at Sturgis for robbing and killing a Meade County rancher.

Perhaps the most contentious criminal court proceeding to occur in the newly created state of South Dakota happened just five years after it had joined the Union, and only four years removed from the massacre at Wounded Knee. That massacre was the result of the rise of the Ghost Dance movement and the death of Sitting

CHIEF TWO STICKS'S DEPARTURE

Bull, the Hunkpapa Lakota leader who had led his band during years of resistance to the policies of the federal government.

It also resulted in the eighth state-sanctioned execution of an individual in the region, with the condemned man being buried in an unmarked Deadwood grave whose location has been lost to time.

The story of Chief Comes Out Holy Two Sticks is one of tragedy, according to Tim Giago, an Oglala Lakota publisher of the *Native Sun News*, founder of the Native American Journalists Association, and a Nieman Fellow at Harvard. Giago contends that many regarded Two Sticks as a great Lakota (Sioux) leader who "became one of the infamous statistics in the wars between the white invaders and the Lakota."

Two Sticks had been at the Greasy Grass with Sitting Bull and Crazy Horse when Yellow Hair and his band of bluecoats were cut down on the rolling bluffs of the Little Big Horn. In the battle's aftermath, he and so many of his brethren resigned themselves to a fate dictated by the Great White Father in Washington, on reservations where there were no more hunts and Indian agents sparingly doled out foodstuffs and government blankets. When it could not get worse it, inevitably, did.

But before the death of a revered warrior or a massacre in the coldest of winters, the advent of the Ghost Dance carried with it the promised return of loved ones departed and a resurgence of the *tatanka* (Lakota for American bison) that had once darkened the plains in a dusty blanket of buffalo sixty million strong.

Two Sticks yearned for that long-gone life of the winter counts, vision quests, and buffalo hunts of his youth. Around him, the world was changing and he knew there was little he could do to alter its course. Soon, two events would set that world of Two Sticks on a tilt from which the old man would never recover.

The first involved Sitting Bull, the Lakota warrior and spiritual leader. Revered for having beaten his enemy, Sitting Bull had toured the world with Buffalo Bill Cody's Wild West Show, and shaken hands with President Grover Cleveland.

December 15, 1890, would harken a change in the federal government's stance, when forty-three Indian police on horseback rode to Sitting Bull's home on the Standing Rock Reservation in northwestern North Dakota.

As authorities attempted to take Sitting Bull into custody, shots were fired and one of those bullets struck the legendary Lakota in the head. Sitting Bull died with his son, Crow Dog, and a dozen other members of his band and law officers.

Two weeks later, on the cusp of 1891, many more would die.

On December 29, along the banks above the frozen waters of Wounded Knee Creek, a band of Lakota comprised of a few warriors, as well as elders, women, and children, were camped. They were surrounded by the remnants of the 7th Cavalry, the same troop nearly annihilated at the Little Big Horn fourteen years earlier.

Errant shots rang out in the encampment that morning, generating a barrage of return fire from the US Army. When the smoke cleared and the dust settled, nearly three hundred Lakota men, women, and children lay dead, with more than fifty wounded, some of whom would later die. Fatalities on the cavalry's side numbered twenty-five, with thirty-nine wounded, six of whom would later die.

CHIEF TWO STICKS'S DEPARTURE

Word of Sitting Bull's death and the massacre of his fellow Indians was slow to filter across the plains. But when it reached Two Sticks's ears, it brought a bitter bile to the back of his throat and reignited a lingering resentment for all that he, and his people, had lost.

Struggling for existence off the reservation in the winter of 1893, the renegade chief found himself traveling with a party of seven consisting of his two sons, Uses a Fight (or Fights With) and First Eagle, as well as a nephew, Kills the Two, and No Water, Hollow Wood, and Whiteface Horses. Together, Chief Two Sticks and his band of bandits roamed the breaks country of southwestern South Dakota, raiding ranches and stealing cattle under the cover of night.

It wasn't long before lawmen, Indian agents, and newspapers took notice of the continuing raids on remote ranches. On February 11, 1893, the *Black Hills Daily Times* described Two Sticks and his associates as "Uncompapas," an unflattering term that implied sneakiness and an underhanded approach to their pursuits.

The article claimed that Uncompapas were the type of Native Americans who, when in council with other Plains Indians, would always position themselves near the exit of the circle so they could flee at the first sign of danger. They were, the newspaper claimed, still nomadic and had remained as uncivilized as they were a century earlier.

That same month, Two Sticks and his band of bandits raided a herd of cattle belonging to Humphrey's cattle ranch, located on the White River a day's ride west of the Pine Ridge Agency. Because Humphrey was raising cows to supply beef to the growing agency, the rancher immediately sent word of the raid to Captain George L. Brown, the acting Indian agent at Pine Ridge. Brown telegraphed soldiers at Fort Meade near present-day Sturgis, advising them to remain on alert for further criminal activity. The 11th Infantry captain then dispatched a half-dozen of his tribal police officers to apprehend the culprits.

When the tribal officers finally located Two Sticks's encampment days later, their attempted apprehension of the criminals did not transpire as planned because the aging chief and his underlings were well armed and ready. When it was over, five tribal police officers were dead and the sixth lay wounded.

Not to be intimidated, and for good measure, Two Sticks and his warriors returned to the Humphrey ranch, site of their earlier crime, and murdered four of its hands: R. Royce, John Bennett, and two youths, identified as thirteen-year-old Charles Bacon and sixteen-year-old William Kelly. Revenge was clearly in evidence by the fact the renegades also shot three horses and thirty cows.

Captain Brown was informed of the killings and, fearful that a Ghost Dance revolt had been initiated, he dispatched a party of twenty-five Indians commanded by tribal policeman Joe Bush after the renegades. Two Sticks and his followers were reportedly holed up at the camp of Chief No Waters and Young Man Afraid of His Horses.

While at the camp of No Waters, Two Sticks purportedly told an Indian man named Crow that the hearts of his young followers were bad and that, during their Ghost Dances, the Great Spirit had told them to kill the whites for their misdeeds of nearly exterminating the buffalo on which they subsisted and stealing their land.

When Bush and his tribal troops arrived at the camp of Chief No Waters and Young Man Afraid of His Horses, Two Sticks and his band of warriors refused to surrender, and a bloody battle was waged. In the initial volley, First Eagle, Kills the Two, and Whiteface Horses were cut down. First Eagle died immediately while others were injured. Two Sticks received a serious bullet wound to his shoulder.

As the rebel leader lay bleeding on the ground, Chief No Waters worked his camp followers into a frenzy and they soon were ready to attack the tribal police. But, Young Man Afraid of His Horses intervened and, in an effort to prevent further bloodshed, the peacemaker and his faithful followers positioned themselves between No Waters's people and the tribal lawmen. When Young Man Afraid of His Horses told No Waters that harming the Indian police in support of the murderers would result in all of their deaths, No Waters backed down.

"The old chief's speech temporarily prevented further bloodshed," author G. Sam Carr wrote in a 2001 article for *Wild West Magazine*. "Still, Captain Brown and others feared that the clash between Two Sticks and the police would arouse the latent fires of rebellion that had been smoldering in the breasts of the Lakota since December 1890. Unless some powerful influence was brought to bear on the disgruntled Indians, the chance of a disastrous outbreak—perhaps even on the scale of the 1890 outbreak that led to Wounded Knee—was great."

To allay the Indians' fears and attempt a nonviolent resolution to the dilemma, Brown assembled more than fifty chiefs at the Pine Ridge Agency on February 6, 1893. During the two-hour meeting, they discussed the murders and Two Sticks's role in the crimes. In the end, most of the chiefs agreed that Two Sticks was a revolutionary who did not share their desire for peace between whites and Indians.

In view of the seriousness of Two Sticks's wounds, police and reservation officials agreed to allow him to recover at the agency before being transported to Deadwood for trial. However, when US Marshal Chris Matthiessen arrived weeks later to take the ailing chief into custody, Two Sticks objected and enlisted No Waters in his cause. The disagreement delayed Two Sticks's departure another month, but when No Waters was arrested, Two Sticks finally gave up his fight and agreed to go to the Black Hills with his compatriots to face justice.

When the marshal finally delivered Two Sticks and his fellow culprits to a jail cell in Deadwood, the chief was reportedly in poor condition, suffered a relapse, and was in a guarded state for several months.

"Two Sticks is wounded in the shoulder, Whiteface Horses in the lower limbs," one observer commented. "Their conditions are loathsome in the extreme. They will not allow a white physician to go near them and their condition can be imagined. Whiteface Horses' legs are gangrened to his knees and his demise is looked for anytime. Two Sticks will probably pull through with the loss of his arm."

Whiteface Horses did later die from his wounds. Following their trials on charges of instigating and conspiring murder and resisting arrest, Hollow Wood, No Waters, and Kills the Two were each sentenced to five years in jail. Hollow Wood and No Waters would die there, but Kills the Two served out his term.

As the leader of the band of cattle rustlers and murderers, Two Sticks was determined by the court to be accountable for the deaths of the four ranch hands and would pay a decidedly more severe penalty: He would be hanged by the neck until dead.

On April 11, 1893, shortly after Two Sticks had been transported to Deadwood, the *Black Hills Daily Times* carried the once-proud Lakota leader's purported confession. It was filled with many regrets for the actions of his boys, still proclaimed his innocence, and showed a measurable amount of remorse that, even at the end, Two Sticks hoped would save him from the gallows. He told a newspaper reporter:

> My friend I have not much to say for my part. I had nothing to do with the killing of the white men. My son that was killed by the Indian police was the cause of all the trouble. I cannot lie, my boy that is dead killed three of the white men and Whiteface Horses killed the other one. I am going to move away. I want . . . and die. My boy (Uses a Fight) that is in jail at Deadwood did not have a gun. He had a bow and arrows. He is only eighteen years old and is a coward. My son that is dead had a rifle. Whiteface Horses had a Winchester. The reason we killed them white men did not treat us right. My son said that he wanted to die and be hung.

As he continued to recuperate from his bullet wound, Two Sticks might have contemplated why the white man's law would help him heal just so it could put him to death.

As Christmas neared, Two Sticks was finally considered well enough to be executed and preparations began in earnest. On December 27, the eve his death sentence would be carried out, Two Sticks appeared calm, according to jailers. He spent the evening alternately sleeping, talking, walking the floor of his cell, and singing. At daybreak, he consumed his last hearty meal of steak grilled over live embers, several slices of bread, and two cups of strong black coffee.

Outside, all was in readiness and a crowd of the curious began assembling in the Lawrence County jail yard at 8:00 a.m. By 9:30, those with tickets were permitted inside an enclosure that consisted of a sixteen-foot-tall solid board fence that spanned the perimeter of the courtyard, keeping prying eyes at bay. At its center stood a solid, albeit hastily constructed gallows. By mid-morning, two hundred people were packed into the enclosure, with many others on the rooftops of surrounding buildings and sheds.

When Two Sticks had finished his meal, Father Digmann and W. L. McLaughlin, the condemned man's attorney, joined the chief and gently informed him that President Cleveland had declined to pardon him for his crimes and that only the gallows and the promise of everlasting life awaited him.

At 9:30, US Marshal Peemiller, accompanied by a gaggle of local officials and newspaper reporters, walked down the corridor to Two Sticks's cell and the death warrant was read aloud, to which the chief merely grunted. When asked if he had any reason the sentence of the court should not be carried out, Two Sticks turned to Peemiller and made a final plea for mercy. He said in a clear voice:

> My heart is not bad. I did not kill the cowboys; the Indian boys killed them. I have killed many Indians, but never killed a white man; I never pulled a gun on a white man. The great father and the men under him should talk to me and I would show them I am innocent. The white men are going to kill me for something I haven't done. I am a great chief myself. I have always been a friend of the white man.
>
> The white men will find out sometime that I am innocent and then they will be sorry they killed me. The great father will be sorry, too, and he will be ashamed. My people will be ashamed, too. My heart is straight and I like everybody. God made all hearts the same. My heart is the same as the white man's. If I had not been innocent, I would not have come up here so good when they wanted me. They know I am innocent or they would not let me go around here. My heart knows I am not guilty and I am happy. I am not afraid to die. I was taught that if I raised my hands to God and told a lie that God would kill me that day. I never told a lie in my life.

Raising both of his hands to the sky, Two Sticks then began his death song. In it, he proclaimed that his heart was good and that God must accept him into his fold when he passed. After the chief had gone on for several minutes and had become increasingly emo-

Chief Two Sticks, seen here in a portrait taken on Christmas Day 1894, was hanged three days later in Deadwood. His place of burial has been lost to history.

COURTESY DEADWOOD HISTORY INC., ADAMS MUSEUM COLLECTION

tional, Father Digmann finally quieted him. Two Sticks turned to the clergyman, grasped his hands, and told him he was a good man.

By some accounts, Two Sticks was then allowed to meet with his wife, a Chinese woman called China Mary. "I'm going to die and go to heaven," Two Sticks told her with sadness in his voice. She curtly replied, "You go to heaven. I'll go to China."

The callousness of his wife's remark may have been too much for the proud Lakota elder. According to witnesses, Two Sticks grabbed a leather strap from a nearby chair, slipped it around his neck, handed one end to another Indian in an adjacent cell and began violently jerking against it. Finally subdued by his jailers and chastised by the clergyman, Two Sticks relented and eventually became resigned to his fate. Growing calm again, he told those in attendance that he was only trying to ensure that if he was to die, he would do so by the hand of his own people, not the white man's.

Marshals then tied his hands behind his back and proceeded slowly to the gallows. Two Sticks walked steadily and, as he left the jail and encountered sunlight for his final time, he examined the courtyard, where he caught his first glimpse of the gallows and all those curious onlookers gathered in their deathly vigil. The chief's only comment was, "Washta you bet," or "Good you bet."

Tired and resigned to his fate, Chief Two Sticks was led up a stairway to the platform of the gallows and placed in his position of honor atop a three-foot-square trap door. As he bowed his head and contemplated the seventy-one winters he had survived on the plains, a clergyman read a short prayer. Then, as a hush fell over the courtyard, Chief Two Sticks raised his head to the heavens and sang his death song once again. Those in attendance were impressed by his steady nerves and strong voice, even as his executioners placed a noose around his neck and placed a black hood over his head.

After an excruciating pause, the crowd heard a grating sound followed by a bang and a loud thud as the trap door opened and Two Sticks fell seven feet, four inches into eternity. At the end of the rope, the chief's neck snapped and death was deemed instantaneous. Nonetheless, he was allowed to hang for fifteen minutes before four local physicians declared him legally deceased and the court's sentence fulfilled.

The body of Two Sticks was placed in a simple pine coffin. His blue leggings and a photograph of him were given to his wife as mementoes; his worn white felt hat was gifted to Sheriff Remer; a red cotton handkerchief presented to his attorney; and his sacred pipe bestowed on Alex Bertrand, a warden who had been friendly with Two Sticks while he was in jail. More than a century later, in October 1998, that *cannumpa* (sacred pipe) would be returned to the family of Two Sticks in a special repatriation ceremony at the Adams Museum in Deadwood, where it had spent decades in the museum's vault.

The remains of Chief Comes Out Holy Two Sticks were interred outside the gates of a local cemetery when the citizens of Deadwood made it clear they did not wish to have the body of an Indian, and a murderer at that, contaminating their graveyard. That final, unmarked resting place has been lost to the ages.

But perhaps the final indignity for the Lakota leader came the next day, December 29, 1894, when the *Black Hills Daily Times* carried a full account of Two Sticks's misdeeds and execution under the headline, "A Good Indian."

CHAPTER 9

The Ghost of W. E. Adams

In Deadwood's infancy, decades before South Dakota joined the Union and long before the gold camp transformed itself from a collection of ramshackle, hastily constructed shacks into the center of commerce for western Dakota Territory, frontier merchants came to the fledgling town in search of their own fortune.

They didn't stand in frigid, knee-deep streams panning for a trace of gold for hours on end like so many hungry prospectors. Instead, these savvy wholesalers, importers, and traders in every manner of merchandise understood that, with a flood of miners, madams, and muleskinners would come demands for supplies ranging from foodstuffs and liquor to hardware, bedpans, and the latest in creature comforts.

Among the first to arrive, just a year into Deadwood's life, was William Emery Adams. He had been born May, 13, 1854, in Bertrand, Michigan, the fifth of nine children born to James and Sarah Ann. Adams later moved to Fairbault, Minnesota, where he and his siblings were reared. No stranger to hard work, he moved to

Minneapolis as a teenager to labor for the American Express Company, which at the time operated as a freighting concern.

But in 1877, soon after his beloved mother had died, Adams heard the call of the West and news of a fabulous gold strike in the Black Hills of Dakota Territory. As was the case with a few thousand like-minded individuals before him, the young man set out for the western wilderness dreaming of hitting it rich with a bit of back-breaking labor and the right mining claim.

Joined by his older brother, James, the twenty-three-year-old Adams quickly quit his job with American Express and headed for the Hills with the Major Whitehead Expedition. Although the younger Adams initially staked a mining claim, with one glance at the sprawling settlement in Deadwood Gulch, with its muddy, bloody Main Street, boisterous saloons, gambling dens and cathouses, and miner's shacks seemingly crawling up every creek-carved canyon in the vicinity, the wiser James eventually convinced his younger brother that their future was probably not tied to the drudgery of panning for color, but was in fact more likely linked to commerce.

Together, the brotherly duo secured a prominent location on the lower end of Main Street and soon constructed a building to house their new business: Banner Grocery Store. Neither of the Adams boys could have known then that their enterprise would exceed their wildest ambitions and lead to a well-heeled life of travel, mansions, philanthropy, and a lasting legacy that would still be lauded more than a century later. Nor could they have known that their life's path would be strewn with unmitigated disaster and personal tragedies so severe that only the strongest would survive.

The Adams brothers did a banner business in groceries their first two years in town, selling everything that muleskinners and their teams of oxen could haul from faraway towns including Pierre, Bismarck, Sidney, and Cheyenne. Produce and milk were delivered by wagon up the hill from nearby Spearfish, where the fertile and well-watered valley kept farmers busy. With so many miners in the northern Black Hills, and new businesses starting up virtually every day, the brothers did all they could to keep their shelves stocked. When it appeared that things could not get any better, they inevitably didn't.

Townspeople went about their business on Thursday, September 25, 1879, enjoying spectacular early fall weather with a warm day followed by the cool mountain air in the evening. Nothing could have signaled what was about to happen in the dead of that night.

At roughly 3:30 a.m., a coal oil lamp dropped from a table in the small Empire Bakery on Sherman Street, just a block from Main Street. The oil splattered the bakery's pine walls, which were lined with canvas, and quickly caught fire, spreading at "an alarming rate."

After the alarm went out, the local fire brigade, the first established in the Black Hills, quickly responded with its hose cart. But this conflagration would soon race to other buildings and nearby houses, erasing them as if they were constructed of paper. The blaze rapidly crossed the street, engulfing the Langrishe Theatre, News and Pioneer, Overland Hotel, Lawrence County Recorder's Offices, and the Jensen and Bliss Hardware Store. It was at the latter location where city officials and local residents knew they had a disaster on their hands, when gunpowder stored in the store exploded, sending a concussion through town and a fireball high into the night sky.

The fire continued its devastating path down Lee Street, eventually arriving at Main Street, where a quickening wind from the southeast sent embers into the air, igniting numerous businesses and, soon, residential homes. While most structures were made of wood, and quickly consumed, not even the brick buildings were immune to the destructive powers of the blaze. The Adams brothers' Banner Grocery was reduced to ashes, and another explosion leveled R. C. Lake's three-story hardware store.

Residents and volunteer firefighters made a gallant effort to contain the inferno, even knocking down buildings to create gaps they hoped the flames would not cross, but Deadwood's Great Fire of 1879 would earn its name.

"It took just three and a half hours to bring the almost total destruction of a city," the *Black Hills Pioneer* would later report. "It was estimated that $2 million [in 1879 valuation] worth of goods and property were destroyed, with 5 million pounds of goods destroyed in the businesses that burned. One death was reported from the fire; an Englishman known as Casino Jack. John King was deaf and already sleeping in Stone's Hotel when the fire broke out. It is believed that because of his hearing deficit, he did not awaken to the alarms."

During the fire, some residents feared it would not be stopped and extend into more of the residential neighborhoods. As a safeguard, many carried their prized possessions into the hills above town.

"In the confusion following the fire, while people searched for friends and family members from whom they had been separated, there was looting and some attempts at claim-jumping," the *Pioneer* reported. County officials closed saloons, as "Men who had not tasted liquor for years imbibed freely to drown their sorrow, and the number of intoxicated men seen on the streets was appalling. Fights were of frequent and hourly occurrence, and disorder and discord was beginning to get possession of the town."

When the fire was finally extinguished about 8:00 a.m., Deadwood residents surveyed a scene of utter and complete devastation. More than three hundred buildings throughout the community had been reduced to piles of ash and rubble. A few who had lost houses to the wildfire packed up whatever they could salvage and left town.

But the majority of Deadwood residents, homeowners and merchants alike, started rebuilding as soon the embers cooled and the last whiffs of smoke were carried away on the wind. William and James Adams were of the latter mindset, intent on building bigger and better, and they were soon constructing a new store across the street from their initial enterprise.

One month after the blaze had leveled virtually the entire business district, beneath the headline, "The fire fiend! Deadwood destroyed," the *Black Hills Daily Times* told a story of recovery.

"A few days over one month ago, the city of Deadwood was visited by fire and almost totally destroyed," reported the November 4, 1879, edition. "Today the city, Phoenix-like, arises from her ashes in more than pristine glory, and is a stable monument to the grit and energy of our citizens."

Back in business in a swanky new store, W. E. Adams, as William came to be known, turned his attention to romance and he began courting Alice Burnham. A few days before Christmas 1880, they were married. Daughter Lucile would be welcomed to the family four years later, while daughter Helen was born in 1892.

Needing more space, the brothers renamed their business to include "Adams Bros." and in the 1880s, successively moved into two larger buildings on Main Street. W. E.'s personal life echoed that business practice, with he and Alice moving several times, in each instance to a more spacious and elegant residence.

By 1894, the Adams brothers began building a new two-story warehouse on Sherman Street. Over the next decade and a half, W. E. would continually expand the structure until it was four stories high, included a water-powered elevator, and had direct access to the Chicago, Burlington and Quincy Railroad. It would eventually become known as the Adams Block Building.

Meanwhile, James Adams was suffering from recurring bouts of an illness, and by 1889, he decided to move to California to improve his health. W. E. bought out his older brother's interest in the business and by the turn of the century, had transitioned the organization from a predominantly retail enterprise into one of the most successful wholesale houses in the state. By 1901, he was operating as the Adams Bros. Wholesale Grocery and Pioneer Fruit Company.

Prominent, successful, happily married and with two grown daughters who had moved from the state, Adams became an ever-present figure in Chamber of Commerce activities and the local Masons, and served as a board member for several local banks and civic organizations. He would eventually serve six terms as mayor of Deadwood, making a variety of improvements that were sometimes funded from his own pocket. Adams erected watering troughs for horses, established a number of city parks, provided American flags for churches and schools, and was credited with laying the first brick streets in Deadwood. The only real loss Adams and his wife experienced was the death of their daughter, Lucile, in 1912, to typhoid fever.

Highly successful, Adams and his wife, Alice, also began spending an increasing amount of time in the colder months living in Pasadena, California, where they eventually built a beautiful residence. The location was extremely popular with South Dakota "snowbirds" trying to escape the state's harsh winter weather.

Described as "both a formidable political opponent and a tender family man," in 1920 Adams decided to purchase one of Deadwood's most luxurious mansions, which had been built by Harris Franklin, one of Deadwood's wealthiest merchants and entrepreneurs. Adams also had run against Franklin for mayor on several occasions, and generally won.

The two-story Queen Anne Victorian mansion had been built in 1893, at a cost of nearly $10,000, and was based on a stock design by the pre-eminent architect Simon Eisendrath. The first floor was built of quarried red sandstone and featured metallic shingles, a third-floor corner turret and dome that served as a smoking room for gentlemen guests, ten spacious rooms, central heat, hot and cold running water, wall-to-wall carpeting, maid calls, electric lights, and telephone service.

According to Mary Kopco, who wrote the book *The Adams House Revealed* in 1896, Franklin engaged a prominent Chicago design firm to add more delicate touches to the mansion.

Lovely, hand-painted, glazed and stenciled canvas-on-plaster wall coverings, stained glass, and decorative painting added even more beauty to this elegant home. The entry hall was given decorative painting of the Empire style, the sitting room was finished in the Flemish Renaissance and the dining room was decoratively painted in the German Baronial. The woodwork in the parlor was painted white enamel and gilt. Beautifully painted clusters of flowers done in watercolors in the corners, which also extended into the center of the ceiling. The room was finished with a beautifully done, stucco cornice of naturally colored flowers and leaves. The stairs off the second-floor sitting room were also added, creating a direct route to the smoking room in the dome.

As soon as they moved in, Adams and Alice immediately took to the expansive residence, hosting dinner parties and afternoon teas. After working so hard for a half-century, Adams was proud of all he had accomplished and wanted his home to reflect everything he had become.

"It was the most prestigious property in Deadwood and it made a major statement," Kopco noted. "W. E. Adams was totally aware of the opulence built into the Franklin House, which had been described in great detail in the local newspapers."

It seemed, for William Emery Adams, that all he had dreamed as a young man had come to fruition. He was at the pinnacle of power and prestige. Everything was in place and all was well. And then suddenly, in just one day, it wasn't.

W. E. Adams, pictured late in life, arrived in Deadwood in 1877 as a twenty-two-year-old would-be miner, but became one of the town's most successful merchants.

In June 1925, Alice, who had been diagnosed with cancer and was being treated, judged herself well enough to travel to California to attend to the birth of their first grandchild. Daughter Helen was seven months pregnant at the time. On June 6, shortly after she had arrived in California, Alice unexpectedly succumbed to her cancer. Distraught over her mother's sudden death, Helen went into early labor and died the following day. The baby, named Helen, lived for only a few hours before also dying.

Adams was rightly devastated and his world unraveled. In the course of only three days, he had lost his wife, his daughter, and his granddaughter. It would take several months before Adams could even discuss the matter. But finally, five months after the deaths, the aging widower sat down and penned the following in the family Bible.

Deadwood, So. Dakota Nov. 15, 1925

W. E. Adams, who married Alice May Burnham December 22, 1880 had hoped we both would live to celebrate our fiftieth anniversary and now, after forty-five years of married life find myself deprived of my loving wife and both of my dear daughters.

I feel like one forsaken and do not see ahead of me in this world much if any happiness. I do hope I shall have the physical & moral strength to follow the teachings of my dear mother who passed from this Earth in 1877 in Minneapolis, Minn., and when I join my wife and daughter in the great unknown I hope none may say with truth I did not keep the faith for their memory is very dear to me.

Dazed and despondent, Adams rambled around his lonely mansion and attended to his mayoral duties and flourishing business for the following year. But clearly the joy in his life had vanished in a scant few days and all of his money and prominence could never bring his loved ones back.

Then, on a long train trip from South Dakota to the comforting sunshine of California, the warmth once again returned to his life. In that passenger car clicking along the westward rails to the Golden State, Adams had an unplanned encounter with an enchanting young widow named Mary Mastrovich Vicich, who had grown up in Lead, Deadwood's sister city, before moving to California at age sixteen. She had married young and, when she was nineteen, her husband had died from influenza.

The unlikely pair immediately hit it off and, through Adams's insistence, began seeing each other with increasing frequency. Following an intense courtship, the two were married in 1927, at the Church of Immaculate Conception in Los Angeles. He was seventy-three. She was twenty-nine.

Adams and Mary would remain married for seven years, splitting their time between mansions in Pasadena and Deadwood. In that time, Mary came to share Adams's love for his adopted home and understand the important role he had come to play in Deadwood's development. She also came to emulate her husband's belief that those best blessed should strive to give back to those less fortunate in their community.

By 1930, Mary Adams had helped convince her husband to build the Adams Memorial Hall Museum as a tribute to his first wife and deceased daughters. Her encouragement resulted in Adams's most enduring legacy—financing the purchase of a lot and construction of the Adams Museum—which still stands today directly across the street from his Adams Block Building.

On June 7, 1934, the eighty-year-old Adams was attending a board meeting at the First National Bank when he suffered a stroke. He died at his home nine days later.

But some say he never really left, and that his spiritual presence remains in Deadwood protecting his beloved home and overseeing his vibrant historical museum.

Following Adams's death, Mary told friends that she had heard her dead husband's footsteps traipsing around the second floor of the mansion. Either out of fear of the unknown or respect for the man with whom she had shared seven years of marriage, Mary closed up the house, leaving everything as it was during their time together.

For the next half-century, the Adams House stood still with time. Original furnishings remained in silence. Linens remained folded, dishes and silverware stayed neatly stacked in cupboards and drawers, and even the cookie jar in the pantry maintained its collection of sweets. Rumors that the house was haunted caused at least two generations of youngsters in the neighborhood to give the stately home a wide berth as they passed on their way to school.

Mary would live to age ninety-three, and each year she would return to Deadwood to visit her mother and entertain friends. But she never stayed in the house again, preferring the Franklin Hotel downtown. In essence, the ghost of W. E. Adams stood guard, protecting the house he and his adoring wife had loved.

And some say he still does.

Late in life, Mary sold the mansion to a couple who operated it as a bed-and-breakfast from 1988 to 1992. When health issues caused them to close the business, the City of Deadwood purchased the property and maintained the B&B until 1995. In 1998, a knowledgeable team of historical experts began work on a complete restoration of the mansion, which they dubbed a "time capsule" and window to the past. Completed with a budget of $1.5 million, the Adams House Museum opened to the public in 2000.

But even before the historic house was used to provide visitors with a glimpse into Deadwood's elegant past, reports of ghostly encounters occurred on a fairly regular basis.

Mary Kopco, who ran W. E. Adams's Museum for nearly two decades, remembers a day in the fall of 1997, when any skepticism about paranormal activities vanished for her and her son. Kopco was living with her husband, Paul, and seven-year-old son, Alex, in the Derosier House next door to the closed-up Adams House. Both of the Kopcos' bedroom windows looked out on the lawn of the adjacent historic home.

"It was late afternoon, Alex was home from school, and I was talking with my sister on the phone," Kopco recalled. "I looked out the window and saw someone, a tall, thin, handsome gentleman, walking back and forth inside what had been Mary Adams's bedroom. I hollered to Alex that someone had broken into the Adams House and he looked out the window and said, 'Don't worry mom. That's Mr. Adams and he likes you.'"

When Kopco mentioned the encounter to a city employee, the woman remarked that she, too, had experienced meeting Mr. Adams, a chance encounter that caused the hair to stand up on the back of her neck. A few days later, Kopco was working at the Adams Museum when she examined a portrait of W. E. Adams. In her mind, she said, "That's the man I saw."

Soon after the historic Adams House opened to the public for tours, docents reported the strange presence of the former business icon who once inhabited the place and, perhaps, still does.

On her first day on the job, one staffer smelled the distinctive aroma of a cigar as she walked the home's second floor. Several others have reported hearing footsteps as they took the stairs to upper levels of the house. One male tour guide was taking a small group through the historic house and when they arrived at Mary's second-floor bedroom, a rocking chair began rocking with no one else around.

"The visitors looked in amazement as did the tour guide, who finally broke the spell by continuing on to the next room, in his professional manner, not letting this manifestation fluster him and disrupt his tour presentation," according to one report.

Whether W. E. Adams's spiritual presence remains in his former residence is a matter of debate. But for Kopco, now executive director of the Fort Collins Symphony in Colorado, a day doesn't pass when she does not think about the success and tragedies of his life, and her own encounter with his mystical existence.

"There were so many little things that happened over the years that were magical," she said. "I still have dreams about W. E. Adams and his wife, Mary. I felt like they were my family and I don't pretend to know where energy goes when people die, but I think his spirit, his energy, is still there protecting the house he loved."

One thing is certain: The legacy of W. E. Adams is found not only at his wonderful museum visited by thousands each year; it's also found in the Adams-Mastrovich Family Foundation, established by Mary before her death. This foundation has doled out hundreds of thousands of dollars over the years to support the arts, education, and religious causes in South Dakota and California.

And, perhaps, the legacy of a man who went west at twenty-two years of age to find fame and fortune, and spent a lifetime helping build a community, raise a family, and, in the process, establish himself as a South Dakota legend, is best exemplified in a simple dedication found at the family mausoleum in a California cemetery, which reads:

> A philanthropist and a friend to all mankind and through whose generosity Adams Memorial Hall was erected in Deadwood, South Dakota, and dedicated to the pioneers of the Black Hills of South Dakota.

CHAPTER 10

The Underground Wilderness

Nearly four million visitors wander the backcountry byways and forested trails of the Black Hills each year, enchanted by a million-acre playground filled with free-roaming wildlife, rippling trout streams, alpine meadows, and what is arguably the highest concentration of parks, monuments, and memorials in the country.

But far below the ponderosa pine forests and grassy mountain meadows of the Black Hills lies an underground wilderness so vast that contemporary explorers are only now beginning to understand its scope and complexity.

In an age when orbiting satellites have mapped the topography of the earth's surface, from its deepest watery recesses to its tallest mountain peaks, subterranean labyrinths such as those found in the Black Hills have become one of the last bastions of mystery in an uncharted terrain.

Often described as one of the last frontiers on the planet, thousands of miles of darkened passageways remain unmapped in

Black Hills caves, corridors that have never felt a human footstep. But, it's not for lack of trying.

Each month year-round, intrepid caving groups descend into the depths of Wind Cave National Park and Jewel Cave National Monument, already two of the world's longest caves, to explore and map more passageways in a tireless effort to find what's actually there. However, none of them expects to ever find the end of the underground trail in their lifetimes.

"It is a mystery in terms of where these holes go," says Tom Farrell, longtime chief of interpretation at Wind Cave National Park. "Will we ever find the end of Wind Cave? At this point, we believe we have as many as 3,000 unexplored holes or passageways, leads that haven't been explored. And, we certainly haven't found the end of it yet."

And, as cave explorers seek to find new passageways in the maze of underground corridors, the going gets tougher, according to experts familiar with the mission and techniques.

"It gets increasingly challenging as they have farther to go each time to reach new passageways," Farrell noted. "Every time you go exploring, if you're on the outer edges, it becomes an increasing distance just to get to the point where you can start new mapping."

Wind Cave National Park, with twenty-eight thousand acres of pine forests, creek-carved canyons, and rolling grasslands above ground, was established in 1903 by President Theodore Roosevelt as the seventh national park in the country. It was the first national park created to protect an underground resource. And what a resource it is.

A National Park Service ranger explains elaborate boxwork formations found in Wind Cave, one of the longest caves in the world. Wind Cave National Park was established in 1903 by President Theodore Roosevelt, the first underground resource protected by the federal government. *Courtesy South Dakota Tourism*

Above ground, more than four hundred bison roam the woodlands and grasslands with large herds of elk and antelope. Below the park's surface lies an incredible maze of 151 miles of mapped passageway, making Wind Cave the third-longest cave in the United States, and the seventh longest in the world.

Farrell says the cave's constant environment of 53 degrees makes Wind Cave a year-round attraction. The fact that it's still largely unexplored makes it a fascinating mystery.

"What has always intrigued me about Wind Cave is its natural opening," Farrell says. "With a change in barometric pressure you can hear a deep, moaning sound that gives you a sense that there's something large down there. The history of the exploration of Wind Cave is filled with one solitary hole leading to miles of passageway. As long as we have one hole that's unexplored, there's a potential for many more miles of cave."

Just nineteen miles away, west of Custer, stands Jewel Cave National Monument. Continuing exploration of Jewel Cave in 1997 moved it from fourth to third longest in the world, surpassing Holloch Cave in Switzerland. During the winter of 2018–19, cave explorers continued mapping passageways in the underground wilderness and surpassed the two-hundred-mile mark. Today, its known passageways are surpassed in length only by Mammoth Cave in Kentucky and Optimisticeskaja Cave in the Ukraine, making Jewel the second longest in the United States and the third longest in the world.

Exploration of Jewel Cave began around 1900 when prospectors Frank and Albert Michaud, joined by friend Charles Bush, heard wind gushing through the rocks in Hell Canyon. Discovering a cave full of sparkling crystals, the trio unsuccessfully attempted to turn the cave into a tourism attraction. In 1908, President Roosevelt protected the unique resource by establishing Jewel Cave National Monument.

As many as eighty thousand visitors enter the 49-degree Jewel Cave during a typical year, taking part in tours ranging from nature talks and lantern walks to four-hour-long Wild Cave adventures. Along the way cavers are treated to some of the rarest cave specimens in the world, including a maze of unusual boxwork, frostwork, and popcorn formations, as well as more common stalactites, stalagmites, and calcite crystals. Dozens of exceedingly rare hydromagnesite balloons—"fragile, silvery little bubbles"—that

A Park Service ranger and his guest are silhouetted in the darkness of Wind Cave, one of the longest caves on earth.

Courtesy South Dakota Tourism

would pop from the mere touch of a finger, are found within Jewel and Wind Caves.

Fifty years after Jewel Cave was designated a national monument, cavers Herb and Jan Conn began a two-decades-long exploration that logged more than six thousand hours and 708 trips into the quiet darkness beneath the Black Hills. The Conns' efforts revealed one of the most extensive and complex cave ecosystems in the world, laced with scientific wonders and scenery few humans had ever encountered.

"The excitement of discovery, the elation and despair. The thrill of pushing forward to discover what is there," Jan Conn wrote in 1975.

That "thrill" of finding the undiscovered continues to motivate a new generation of cavers hell-bent on mapping the next mile of unexplored passageway, because there could be hundreds of miles of virgin corridors that have never felt a human presence. In fact, air-column studies conducted by scientists indicate that which is known to exist in Wind and Jewel Caves may constitute less than 10 percent of what is actually there.

Based on the barometric pressure outside, air either enters or leaves a cave. Using computer modeling, scientists have recorded data on the amount of air entering or exiting these two caves and come to the conclusion that the mapped passageway may be just 5–10 percent of the void that truly makes up these miraculous, dark, dank caverns.

"Imagine, Wind and Jewel Caves are nineteen air-miles apart, but perhaps they could be connected," Farrell speculated. As another National Park Service ranger at Jewel Cave said, "We've mapped the ocean floor, but we probably have thousands of miles of cave passages that we have not yet found."

Yet, features of the underground wilderness found at Wind and Jewel Caves are not confined to stalagmites, stalactites, boxwork, and tiny, fragile balloons. Other features in the caves have allowed park rangers and scientists to better understand the world that resides below.

Some 450 feet below the earth's surface at Wind Cave is Windy City Lake, a tranquil body of water on which float small calcite rafts. Through carbon dating, monitoring, and other scientific techniques, scientists have confirmed the small underground lake is directly tied into the Madison Aquifer, which flows under the vast majority of western South Dakota. After an extremely wet spring and early summer in 2019, cave management specialists reported that water levels at the lake were within one inch of the highest level ever recorded.

As the United States celebrated the fiftieth anniversary of landing a man on the moon in 2019, and pondered a return, as well as a new mission to Mars, some remain transfixed with what exists in the depths below. "Caves are a whole other world," the Jewel Cave ranger said. "Rarely do we get to explore the underground wilderness—a world that is always under our feet."

CHAPTER 11

An Unsolved Murder

It's been nearly a century since a dynamite explosion rocked a quiet Deadwood neighborhood, leaving a respected civil servant dying in a pool of his own blood, and shattering windows and the serene sense of safety that touched nearly all of the town's residents in the bucolic 1920s.

Certainly, Deadwood was no stranger to murder. After all, famed western scout and former lawman James Butler "Wild Bill" Hickok became the town's most famous permanent resident when a miscreant named "Crooked Nose" Jack McCall, seeking some personal notoriety, snuck up behind Hickok and shot him in the back of the head while he was playing poker in a Deadwood saloon shortly after his arrival in August 1876. Hickok fell forward onto the poker table, spilling aces and eights, forever after known as "the Deadman's Hand."

McCall was tried by a "miner's court" in Deadwood, which failed to find him guilty. But the no-account drifter was later arrested by a US marshal in Cheyenne, Wyoming, after bragging in a bar about gunning down the legendary figure. He was transported to the Dakota territorial capital in Yankton, where he was tried again, found guilty, and summarily hanged, then buried in an unmarked grave.

In the race for riches in Deadwood's early gold rush years, the town's homicide rate was unusually high, spurred on by claim jumpers, highwaymen, bandits, cutthroats, and cattle thieves all seeking their fortunes from the labors of others.

But, other than the unfortunate murder of Preacher Henry Weston Smith, killed outside Deadwood as he walked to give a sermon to the wayward in a neighboring gold mining camp just days after Hickok's death, the vast majority of crimes and killings in the fabled gulch were eventually solved, the perpetrator consigned to a jail cell or simply dropped, a sturdy rope around the neck, from a quickly constructed gallows near the courthouse downtown.

Commonly, those early-day deaths came from a six-gun, but following the start of the twentieth century, those were relatively rare. In fact, by the 1920s, Deadwood was the center of commerce in western South Dakota, boasting railroads, a theater, and the mile-deep Homestake Gold Mine up the hill in Lead, which employed hundreds.

The town was filled with modern conveniences that generally took far longer to follow the plow across the prairies and reach the remote villages and townships of the Midwest, including trolleys, gas street lights, and telephone service that arrived in Deadwood the same year it was installed in the White House. Certainly, by the 1920s, the gunslingers had vanished and the quickly constructed frontier facades had been replaced by Victorian storefronts built from bricks and stone, while the muddy and sometimes bloody thoroughfares were supplanted by brick-lined streets.

Arguably, the worst characters to inhabit the once wild and wooly place in the early 1900s were bootleggers, prostitutes, and dealers who shuffled cards in smoky backroom poker games—all of whom had the unofficial blessing of city fathers and local lawmen. Remarkably, those upstairs brothels would continue to operate above Deadwood's busy Main Street until federal authorities closed them down during raids in May 1980. And, advocates of the painted ladies will tell you, the Black Hills deer hunting season has never been quite the same.

It was during this period and the decade before that the skills of Frank Peck would become readily apparent. Peck was born December 19, 1861, in Nodaway, Missouri, before moving with his parents to Deadwood in 1878. In 1891 he married Martha Baxter, who had moved to Deadwood in 1890 from Savannah, a small town in northwestern Missouri just a few miles from Peck's birthplace. The couple made their home at 37 Charles Street on Deadwood's south side, as Frank continued his career as a civil engineer.

There was no shortage of business in the vibrant region. The Homestake Gold Mine, owned by George Hearst and, subsequently, his son William Randolph Hearst, had been in operation since 1877, and would eventually extract some $1.2 billion in bullion before finally closing in 2002. By the time Peck arrived on the scene, his services were in great demand.

By 1904, Peck had compiled a comprehensive map of all the mining claims in the northern Black Hills, a document that historians have since labeled "the bible" for land claims.

Automobiles, whose ownership was once limited to the well heeled, were becoming an everyday necessity for the average resident, and the region's mining, timber, and cattle industries were quickly making way for a burgeoning tourism business in the Black Hills, thanks to hundreds of miles of newly constructed roads.

While Peck's early work relied on the largesse of massive mining operations in the Hills, it evolved in scope, and soon Peck was tapped to assist in surveying the northern border of South Dakota. His expertise drew the attention of the state's governor, who appointed Peck to the state examining board for engineers.

In his off hours, Peck was intimately involved in community affairs, with membership in at least five civic organizations, including the Shriners and Elks. He also served as a volunteer for the Deadwood Hose Company as a young man, and later transferred to the Homestake Hose Company. He remained a firefighter for the rest of his life.

While sculptor Gutzon Borglum wouldn't begin carving the four faces of freedom on Mount Rushmore National Memorial until 1927, a work that would consume the last fourteen years of his life and create one of America's most iconic symbols, early tourism advocates believed the hospitality industry was key to a brighter future, and pushed for building paved highways and scenic byways then in demand throughout the country. Understanding that mandate, Peck quickly turned his attention to road building.

Among his friends was W. E. Adams, a wealthy Deadwood merchant and benefactor who would later gift an entire museum to the town. Together, the pair surveyed a new road between Deadwood and its northerly neighbor, Spearfish. The project brought

AN UNSOLVED MURDER

Peck further attention, leading the *Deadwood Daily Pioneer-Times* to label him "The pioneer road engineer of the state."

In 1926, Peck was working as highway superintendent for Lawrence County, a prestigious position with perks that included a five-passenger Studebaker touring sedan, which he drove to work each day. Even though it was Labor Day, Monday, September 6, Peck went about his regular routine, awaking at 5:30 or 6:00 a.m., and departing for work about 7:00. His wife, Martha, later reported that her husband had gathered a basket of laundry and walked across the street from their house on Charles Street to the garage in which he kept his prized car.

While opening the garage door, Peck noticed a tire pump, plunger extended, laying amidst some vegetation in the driveway. After setting the clothes basket in the vehicle, he went back to check the tire pump, either inspecting its operation or to see if it held any identifying marks that would indicate its ownership. Knowing that his own tire pump was safely stored in the trunk of his own Studebaker, Peck likely assumed it had been discarded by a neighbor. So, he probably decided to simply put it away for safe-keeping. He grabbed the device, put it in the middle of his driveway in front of the garage, placed it between his feet, and depressed the plunger.

The resultant explosion would rock the Deadwood community, send shockwaves through the neighborhood, shatter windows, and eventually end Peck's life. The blast sent Peck several feet backwards, cratered his driveway, and changed all that had come before.

Martha heard the blast from the house and came running across the street, only to find her loving husband on the ground, bleeding profusely, and in danger of losing his life. She immediately ran back to the house and dialed St. Joseph's Hospital, which was less than a block away.

Doc Thorpe, a plumber who lived a couple of doors down at 21 Charles Street, rushed to the scene and found his injured neighbor alive, conscious, and aware of what was happening.

"He was laying on his back moaning and I asked him what had happened, and he said he got blowed up," Thorpe would later testify. "I asked him who done it, and he said, 'I don't know who could do a thing like this,' and he repeated that several times. He wanted me to help him raise his head so that he could look at his feet and he said, 'I am going to bleed to death if we don't get this blood stopped,' and then I tied up his limb above the knee and we stopped the blood."

In his valiant effort to save his neighbor, Thorpe was joined by James Pence, a foreman at the Chicago, Burlington & Quincy Railroad roundhouse located just behind Peck's garage.

"When the explosion came I was standing in my office door," Pence later testified in court. "I ran across as fast as I could. Mr. Peck told (me), 'Oh my God, I don't know what I have ever done to plant this machine for me.'"

Assistance soon arrived, and Peck was carried on a stretcher to the nearby hospital. Frank Howe, the town's mayor and an eminent physician, attended to Peck's wounds. The doctor immediately amputated Frank's right foot, then realizing that the real immediate danger to Peck's life was shock, elected to forego further treatment for a day. However, on Wednesday, Dr. Howe amputated Peck's left leg.

Frank Peck was a respected Deadwood surveyor and Lawrence County official at the time of his death in 1926. His ghastly murder caused by an improvised explosive device has never been solved.

COURTESY DEADWOOD HISTORY INC., ADAMS MUSEUM COLLECTION

"He seemed to rally and get better," the physician would later testify before a packed courtroom. "He got off the table in good shape but at times he was bad. He was in fairly good condition and seemed better for the rest of the day, and later on Thursday complications arose—intestinal and stomach complications—which were serious, getting more serious until his death."

At 10:40 a.m. on Friday, September 10, Frank Peck took his last breath. With word of his passing, an untold tragedy befalling the otherwise calm community of Deadwood, all flags were lowered to half-mast for the remainder of the day.

With the death of a highly respected county official, law enforcement investigators sprang into action, as did the media.

"This was a high-profile crime, one that prompted headlines in the *Deadwood Daily Pioneer-Times* that read 'Dastardly Attempted Assassination: Road Supervisor Peck Frightfully Mutilated by a Murderer's Bomb,' and 'Frank Peck Has Lost in the Gallant Fight Which He Made for His Life,'" Dustin Floyd wrote in a March 2006 edition of *Deadwood Magazine*. "The Deadwood Police Department and the Lawrence County Sheriff were quick to investigate the murder, but few records of their work survive, due in part to a fire that destroyed Deadwood City Hall in 1952," Floyd continued.

But Floyd's own probe, conducted nearly eighty years after the murder of Frank Peck, discovered valuable and illuminating documents in the City of Deadwood archives. Among the most critical was a transcript of a two-day hearing that took place on September 24-25 after police had charged Rudolph Fredericks, a former county road worker who had had a disagreement with Peck, with the man's horrific murder.

Although police had recovered the remains of the tire pump, the murder weapon that had resulted in Peck's death, it proved nearly impossible to connect the device with Fredericks. Investigators did, however, determine from firsthand accounts of the blast that the explosive used in the tire pump was likely dynamite, of which Fredericks had recently purchased several sticks.

Law enforcement investigators also documented that Fredericks had several "heated exchanges" with Peck on at least two occasions prior to the incident. The first had occurred in February 1926, shortly after an accidental explosion on a road project in Boulder Canyon, immediately north of Deadwood, had killed one of Fredericks's brothers and injured another.

"They were all working on the same county road crew at the time, and Fredericks resigned until Lawrence County paid adequate compensation," Floyd wrote. "When the process didn't move fast enough, Fredericks publicly made his displeasure known to Frank."

An even more intense encounter occurred in August of the same year, precipitated by Peck presenting Fredericks with a bill for the use of county road equipment on the latter's family ranch. Livid over the $29.75 invoice, Fredericks marched into Peck's office in the courthouse basement and confronted the county road superintendent over the matter. An unfortunate county official who stumbled on the encounter testified that it looked as if Fredericks was close to becoming violent with Peck.

Perhaps the most compelling evidence against Fredericks, however, came from a neighbor of the Pecks, Fred Conard, who testified that on the night prior to the explosion that took Frank Peck's life, he witnessed a Studebaker roadster stop near the Peck garage. Conard said he became suspicious when the car's driver raced back to his vehicle in an "excited" manner and drove off quickly. His description closely resembled the car commonly driven by Fredericks who, police noted, had no verifiable alibi for the evening of the incident. Sadly, under sworn testimony, the elderly neighbor noted that he had not noticed the vehicle's license plate number.

When the court hearing was eventually convened in September 1926, prosecutors faced an uphill battle armed with what was, at best, circumstantial evidence against Fredericks. Much of the investigators' evidence had been destroyed in the aftermath of the explosion.

"Fingerprinting was relatively common by the 1920s, but the murder weapon—the modified tire pump—had been immediately seized and handled by the curious crowd that gathered at the scene," Floyd wrote. "A narrow passageway near the garage that was the murderer's likely route was filled with fresh mud, but police didn't check for footprints until after the crowd had trampled the earth into a sloppy mess."

After the judge had heard the testimony of seventeen witnesses, on September 25, he ruled that the case would proceed to trial in early December in Deadwood's Eighth Circuit Court. While the ruling gave prosecutors two additional months to gather evidence, today no one truly knows what transpired at that trial as transcripts of the proceeding have been lost to time.

AN UNSOLVED MURDER

According to Floyd's exhaustive study, the next surviving record of the case is a criminal dismissal order dated June 7, 1929, clearing Fredericks of the crime and allowing him to walk free.

But Lawrence County sheriff William Remer's personal journal illuminates the length investigators went to find Peck's killer. That journal reveals that detectives had identified at least two other potential suspects in the murder, although no legal action was ever levied against the individuals. Despite an offer of a $500 reward to anyone who helped nab the killer, there were no other arrests in the case.

However, in a subsequent journal entry dated February 11, 1938, a dozen years after the explosion that rocked Deadwood and killed Peck, Remer wrote, "Ross Dunn gave me inside history of Frank Peck's death. Is positive it was Fredericks."

Nonetheless, no one was ever convicted of killing the respected Deadwood citizen and county official, and the person responsible for his death remains one of the fabled town's enduring mysteries. Today, Peck Street on the city's south side is a reminder of the esteem in which he was held.

If you walk into Deadwood City Hall, you'll discover a beautiful Eureka Safe & Lock Company safe, circa 1895, in which the murdered man once stored his most precious possessions. Across the face of this stunning safe is painted the name "Frank S. Peck."

Chapter 12

The Jackalope: South Dakota's Scariest Rabbit

Of all the critters that claim South Dakota as home, among the rarest and certainly the scariest is the western jackalope, an aggressive species of male jackrabbit mated with a female antelope. Willing to use its antlers to ward off attacking predators, accounts of this unusual specimen, also known as the "warrior rabbit," date back centuries, but first came to be known in the Old West when frontier trappers and cattlemen made their initial encounters.

The legend of the jackalope, arguably the most iconic American creature next to Bigfoot, can be found in works dating to the 1200s, when a rabbit with a single unicorn-like appendage appeared in a Persian geographic dictionary, and to the late 1700s, when a horned hare was depicted in a European work of natural history.

The freakish "Frankenstein" rabbit may also be found in the Smithsonian Institution's National Museum of Natural History, where the horny facial growths of a cottontail rabbit have been attributed to the Shope papilloma virus. According to the Smithsonian, the unusual "virus infects rabbits and hares worldwide, causing tumors to grow in various places on the rabbit's head and body."

Offspring of the horned hare also seem to have hopped to Europe, where in Germany the creature is known as the *wolpertinger*, and in Sweden where it's commonly called the *skvader*. But nowhere is the legend of the jackalope more prevalent than in the American West, where the strange critter is ubiquitous throughout South Dakota, Wyoming, Colorado, New Mexico, and other rural states, appearing as wall mounts in saloons, hotels, and souvenir shops.

Rarely seen alive and variously attributed to a cross between a now-extinct pygmy deer and a startling dangerous species of killer-rabbit, the first jackalope in the American West was reportedly captured by an "occasionally sober trapper" named Roy Ball in 1829. Others contend that Ball, owner of the LaBonte Hotel in Douglas, Wyoming, actually purchased a jackrabbit carcass to which two brothers had attached a small set of deer antlers for the ungodly price of $10—nearly $200 by today's standards. Nonetheless, when Ball displayed the jackalope mount in his hotel, the attraction reportedly created a sensation.

By other accounts, brothers Douglas and Ralph Herrick of Douglas accidentally created the mythical creature in 1939, following a day of hunting. Ralph had thrown a dead jackrabbit on the floor of their shop, where it slid right up against a pair of deer antlers. He then exclaimed, "It looks like a rabbit with horns on it." Shortly thereafter, Douglas, who worked as a taxidermist, began

While jackalope mounts are ubiquitous in parts of the West, sightings of the fearsome creature in the wild are few and far between.

churning out the unlikely mounts and began selling them to a welcoming public.

Soon, the jackalopes were everywhere: in homes and taverns and even on postcards. By the late 1940s, Douglas had proclaimed itself as the "Jackalope Capital of the World," and the town still celebrates the strange conception with Jackalope Days every June.

Perhaps the strangest offshoot of the whole enterprise is the availability of a limited, non-resident jackalope license, which the Converse County Chamber of Commerce has issued by the thousands. Strangely, the rules state that the hunter may not have an IQ higher than 72, can hunt only between midnight and 2:00 a.m. each June 31st, and must be a person of "strict temperance and absolute truthfulness." If interrogated concerning their hunting experience, the license also requires the holder, "to employ such lingual evasion, loud rebuttal and double talk as the occasion and circumstances require."

Soon after the Herrick brothers perpetuated the myth, jackalopes would be spotted in South Dakota, roaming the ragged ridgelines and sawtooth spires of the Badlands and sneaking through the dark ponderosa pine forests and creek-carved canyons of the Black Hills.

Some early-day observers claimed the wily jackalope possessed an uncanny ability to mimic human sounds. When open-range cowboys settled in by the campfire at night, singing their favorite tunes with the call of coyotes echoing across the grasslands, jackalopes could frequently be heard singing back, mimicking the refrains of the cowboys. For many, this creature with the elongated horns protruding from its furry little head remains the stuff of nightmares; for others, it's just a mythological rabbit with outlandish habits and a host of campfire stories to back it up.

When confronted, this antlered species of rabbit, described by those in the know as brownish in color, weighing between three and five pounds, and moving at "lightning speeds" approaching 90 miles per hour, can be vicious, using their antlers to ward off predators in a fight to the death.

Although its small head and spiky antlers made the creature look fairly docile, those who had early encounters with the animal quickly became aware that it could be a dangerous and potentially deadly adversary. While some noted that jackalopes could move extremely fast when being pursued, leaving only a trail of dust in their wake, others reported that the horn-headed rabbit sometimes preferred to square off with a foe, often with injurious results. When striking its defensive posture, the jackalope would lower its sharp spikes and charge its enemy, leaving deep gouges and bloody wounds in any challenger. That tendency eventually led jackalope hunters to wear stove pipes over their legs when tracking the furry beasts.

It also has been said that many Black Hills deer hunters, who roam the forests, alpine meadows, and foothills in search of their elusive trophy each fall, always carry a canteen of their finest whiskey in case they encounter a jackalope. Apparently, despite its fierce tendencies, it's rumored that the crafty creature carries such an acquired taste for the distilled spirit that it can be willingly persuaded to come close to a human—and even be captured—with just one sip.

Those few brave jackalope hunters who were successful in capturing their prey alive claimed that the milk of the female jackalope was extremely valuable because it could cure most illnesses. However, those claims were quickly debunked when the hunters were unable, or unwilling, to describe just how one milked such a dangerous animal in captivity.

Whether jackalopes are real, sneaking through the darkness of night just outside the twinkling light of a camper's wood fire, or merely an enduring legend and the result of an over-active imagination, time will tell.

But sing a ditty while sitting around the campfire at night and wait for the return refrain, or wander through famed attractions like the Wall Drug Store near Badlands National Park, and you're likely to encounter a beautiful mount of this unusual jackrabbit with its foreboding antlers. And with time, you may add to the growing litany of strange stories and mysterious tales tied to one of the wonders of the West.

Chapter 13

Gutzon Borglum: One Man's Mountain

As thousands of visitors walk through the Avenue of Flags on any given sunny summer afternoon and out onto the vast grand view terrace at Mount Rushmore National Memorial, they are greeted by the giant likenesses of four great US presidents: George Washington, Thomas Jefferson, Abraham Lincoln, and Theodore Roosevelt.

Most stand in awe of the largest work of art on earth, speaking in whispers as if in a church, reveling in the specter of granite giants representing the birth, growth, preservation, and development of the United States of America.

But, had it not been for one man who knew what America had to say and the scale on which to express it, Mount Rushmore's nearly three million annual visitors might instead be staring at the carved figures of western heroes such as Buffalo Bill Cody, Jim Bridger, Lewis and Clark, and Sacagawea.

For it was a distinctly American sculptor known as Gutzon Borglum who ultimately decided that backers of a proposed mountain carving in South Dakota's fabled Black Hills needed to "pitch the note high enough" to enlist the support of an entire nation and create a monument for the ages.

Doane Robinson, secretary and superintendent of the South Dakota State Historical Society, is credited with the idea for a mountain memorial. He first broached the subject with US senator Peter Norbeck in December 1923. Robinson contended that a Black Hills memorial on the epic scale of Egypt's Sphinx would foster national attention for the region and eventually bring millions of dollars to the state's burgeoning tourism industry.

When Robinson contacted artist Gutzon Borglum about the concept in the summer of 1924, his idea could not have come at a more opportune moment for the beleaguered sculptor.

"In the vicinity of Harney Peak in the Black Hills of South Dakota are opportunities for heroic sculpture of unusual character," Robinson wrote to Borglum on August 20. "Would it be possible for you to design and supervise a massive sculpture there? The proposal has not passed beyond mere suggestion, but if it would be possible for you to undertake the matter I feel quite sure we could arrange to finance such an enterprise."

At the time Borglum received Robinson's note, the artist was toiling on a monument to the Confederacy at Stone Mountain, Georgia, and the work was not going well. In the midst of a contentious relationship with that memorial's backers, one that would eventually lead to Borglum destroying his models, abandoning the project, and fleeing the state with authorities in hot pursuit, Robinson's welcome invitation arrived.

In fact, Borglum was so enthused by the prospect of Robinson's plan and so frustrated by his relationship with the Stone Mountain Confederate Memorial Association, he wired a response to Robinson within hours stating, in part, "Very much interested in your proposal. Great scheme you have. Hold to it. The North will welcome it."

The next month, Borglum and his young son, Lincoln, found themselves in the emerald oasis of the Black Hills, surveying a scene of wonder and one of the most ancient mountain ranges in the world.

"I know of no group of rock formations that equals those found in the Black Hills," Borglum told a local newspaper reporter on that initial visit, "nor any that is so suitable to sculpture."

The fifty-seven-year-old sculptor already was world-famous when he arrived in Rapid City in 1924. Born in Ovid, Idaho—then the western frontier—on March 25, 1867, Borglum was the son of Danish immigrants. His introduction to the world of art began at sixteen, when he became an apprentice to a lithographer in California. When Borglum was only twenty-one years old, his painting of the famed explorer and cartographer General John Charles Fremont was well received and set him on a path for a career in art.

By 1890, Borglum was studying in Paris under celebrated French sculptor Auguste Rodin, a tutelage that led to high-dollar commissions throughout Europe and the United States. In the succeeding decades, as his reputation grew, his career flourished, as did his earnings and his ego. Evidence of his productivity during those years is best found at Statuary Hall in the US Capitol in

Mount Rushmore sculptor John Gutzon de la Mothe Borglum

Washington, DC, where more of Borglum's work is on display than that of any other artist.

Arguably, Borglum's only real career setback occurred at Stone Mountain, when a disagreement between the artist and the association that had hired him led its board to vote to dismiss Borglum and hire another artist to complete the work according to his detailed plans. The recalcitrant Borglum subsequently rushed to Atlanta, raced to the top of Stone Mountain, and personally pushed his working models over the side of the cliff, destroying them on the rocks far below.

While Borglum's years of work on Stone Mountain were eventually blasted and drilled away, to be replaced by the creation of another artist, Borglum did carry with him from Georgia a mountain of experience in carving on a colossal scale that would prove invaluable as he tackled the granite cliff in the Black Hills that would consume the remaining years of his life.

After surveying several sites on horseback in the Black Hills in August of 1925, Borglum settled on a remote granite outcropping in the central Hills known as Mount Rushmore for his mammoth mountain memorial. Years earlier, after the great gold rush of 1876, the little-known crag had been named for New York City attorney Charles E. Rushmore, who had assisted Black Hills miners with a series of claims in 1884 and 1885.

After climbing to its summit, sampling its rock, and surveying its surroundings, Borglum believed the mountain was best suited for his mission due to its mass, which could support a sculpture of monumental scale, and its south-easterly exposure, which would gather the sun's rays and spotlight his work for the majority of each day.

"Here is the place," Borglum exclaimed. "American history shall march across that skyline."

As Mount Rushmore backers spent the next two years identifying funding sources and getting legislation passed that would allow for such a mountain carving, Borglum and his sponsors held seemingly endless discussions and correspondence over the subject of his work. The noted artist quickly rejected Robinson's initial suggestion of western characters, believing that a memorial dedicated to the ideals of democracy depicted through four great leaders was a better concept that could be embraced by every American.

Eventually, per Borglum's strong suggestion, the visages of Washington, Jefferson, Lincoln, and Roosevelt were selected. As father of the country, Washington was chosen because he was an individual of unquestionable integrity, had led the nation in its infancy, and, by refusing to wear a crown, helped determine that the country would be a representative democracy. Jefferson was selected not for his authorship of the Declaration of Independence drafted at age thirty-three, or his two terms as the third president of the United States, but for his vision of a nation that spanned from sea to sea. Specifically, Borglum cited Jefferson's 1803 purchase of the Louisiana Territory from French general Napoleon Bonaparte, which more than doubled the size of the United States, and is still regarded as the best real estate transaction of all time.

As was the case with most sculptors of this era, Abraham Lincoln held a special place in Borglum's heart. His heralded bust of the Great Emancipator remains on permanent display in the rotunda of the US Capitol and was so celebrated that when it was unveiled, Lincoln's son, Robert Todd Lincoln, reportedly said,

"I never thought I would see father again." So esteemed was the nation's sixteenth president to Borglum, that he gave his only son his name. There was little disagreement when Borglum chose Lincoln for Mount Rushmore, all knowing that he had held the nation together in the throes of a bloody Civil War.

In fact, the only dissension to Borglum's selections for Mount Rushmore came when he announced that Theodore Roosevelt would be included in the venerated foursome. A personal friend of the twenty-sixth president, Borglum had served as Roosevelt's Connecticut campaign chairman and had personally visited him at the White House on numerous occasions. While historians objected, contending that history had not yet had time to judge Roosevelt's presidency just eight years after his death, Borglum prevailed, noting it was Roosevelt's Panama Canal that had "joined the waters of the great East and West seas," completing the dream of Columbus and allowing the United States to exert its naval influence around the world.

But selecting the subjects for Mount Rushmore would prove relatively simple when compared with the back-breaking work that would command the remaining years of Borglum's life. Fortunately, an unpredictable visit and endorsement from a sitting president, as well as the tireless efforts of the Mount Rushmore National Memorial Society, would aid Borglum in overcoming seemingly insurmountable financial and logistical obstacles in creating a memorial that would stand for all time.

Thanks to the urging of Senator Norbeck, President Calvin Coolidge selected the Black Hills for his summer vacation in 1927, choosing the State Game Lodge in Custer State Park for his sojourn. Coolidge and First Lady Grace found the mountain air soothed "Silent Cal's" bronchitis, and he soon began relishing trout fishing in a small brook next to the lodge that had been well stocked with trout by local ambassadors. In short order, the president's planned three-week vacation turned into a three-month stay.

Although Coolidge had initially stated he would make no public appearances during his visit, the extended holiday soon found the president and his entourage attending Sunday services at a small church in Hermosa, donning a Native American headdress at Deadwood's Days of '76 celebration, and entertaining several invitations to visit a yet-to-be-commenced mountain carving in the middle of nowhere. Perhaps Borglum's unusual welcoming in which he hired a pilot to fly a biplane over the State Game Lodge, where he dropped a wreath for the president, had something to do with Coolidge finally accepting an invite to Mount Rushmore.

Supporters of the mountain memorial were delighted on August 10, 1927, when President Coolidge finally arrived at Mount Rushmore with his Secret Service contingent in tow, all on horseback, because no road yet reached the secluded venue. More than a thousand South Dakotans were on hand to see Coolidge dedicate the new monument, and when the president walked to the edge of a hastily constructed platform, grabbed a ladle from a common pail of water and took a drink, they knew the Vermont farm boy was their kind of guy.

But no one, Borglum included, could have predicted what Coolidge would say, and when he said it, no supporter of this new mountain memorial could believe he had.

"We have come here to dedicate a cornerstone laid by the hand of the Almighty," Coolidge told the assembled crowd. Then, he became the first government official to refer to Mount Rushmore as a "national shrine," and most importantly, one deserving of the federal government's support. With that, Borglum raced to the top of the mountain and used six drill bits to symbolically start carving the Washington figure on the face of what Franklin Delano Roosevelt would later define as "America's Shrine of Democracy."

Despite the stated intent, it would take another eighteen months before Coolidge, in one of his final acts as president in February 1929, signed a federal appropriation for Mount Rushmore. While the memorial's small cadre of supporters worked to raise funds to match the federal dollars flowing to the project, that summer Borglum enlisted the help of dozens of Black Hills miners, many unemployed by the advent of the Great Depression, to build a studio, roads, walls, and buildings, and then he began carving in earnest on America's newest mountain memorial.

On July 4, 1930, a scant year after carving truly began, a crowd of locals and tourists attracted to the unusual undertaking gathered to hear a twenty-one-gun salute and celebrate the unveiling of Washington's likeness on Mount Rushmore, which had been draped by an enormous American flag stitched together by local women.

Over the ensuing eleven years, three other dedications would take place, revealing the six-story portraits of Jefferson, Lincoln, and Roosevelt.

After being asked by thousands of visitors, as well as newsreel and newspaper reporters, about what he was attempting to create on a mountain in the middle of America, midway through the carving Borglum sat down and penned his mission statement. It read:

> We are not here trying to carve an epic, portray a moonlight scene, or write a sonnet; neither are we dealing with mystery or tragedy, but rather the constructive and dramatic moments or crises in our amazing history.
>
> We are cool-headedly, clear-mindedly setting down a few crucial, epochal facts regarding the accomplishments of the Old World radicals who shook off the shackles of oppression from their light feet and fled despotism to people a continent; who built an empire and rewrote the philosophy of freedom and compelled the world to accept its wiser, happier form of government.
>
> Therefore, we believe a nation's memorial should, like Washington, Jefferson, Lincoln and Roosevelt, have a serenity, a nobility, a power that reflects the gods who inspired them and suggests the gods they have become.
>
> Hence, let us place there, carved high, as close to heaven as we can, the words of our leaders, their faces, to show posterity what manner of men they were. Then breathe a prayer that these records will endure until the wind and the rain alone shall wear them away.

All told, nearly four hundred men and a few women would work on the memorial or on behalf of Borglum at the mountain. The most skilled drillers and powdermen relied on experience gleaned from years working in gold mines in the Black Hills, as well as the techniques Borglum had acquired in his time at Stone Mountain. Powdermen, who followed drillers along the mountain each day, filling their granite holes with precise amounts of dynamite, became so adept at their trade that they could block out a nose, mouth, cheeks or brows within inches of the finished surface. Finish drillers would follow, suspended in bosun chairs affixed to winches atop the mountain, "honeycombing" the remaining rock to be removed. Once the excess rock had been wedged and hammered off the face, "four-star" bumping bits would be employed to put the final touches on the sculpture, leaving the rock as smooth as a newly poured sidewalk.

Due to Borglum's attention to safety on site (he would personally check cables each morning and have them replaced if even a few strands were broken), no workers died in the fourteen years of construction of Mount Rushmore. By comparison, a dozen workers died in eighteen months during the Las Vegas construction boom of the early 2000s.

Each of the heads stand sixty feet tall, with approximately twenty-one-foot-tall noses, eleven-foot-wide eyes, and eighteen-foot-wide mouths. Once asked how tall the presidents would have been had they been carved from head to heel, Borglum suggested 365 feet tall, then added they would be able to wade the Potomac River without getting their knees wet and would have had to kneel down to read by the light from the torch of the Statue of Liberty.

Perhaps Borglum's greatest artistic feat at Mount Rushmore remains the eyes of each president, which seem to follow a visitor as they stroll around the memorial. Each iris was sculpted as a hole, while a protruding cube of granite was retained in each to catch reflected light, leaving a realistic appearance unequaled by the great Roman, Greek, and Italian sculptors.

Often delayed by severe winter weather, summer thunderstorms, and a lack of funding, progress on the memorial nonetheless continued. All told, six and a half years of actual work occurred during a fourteen-year span from 1927 to 1941, continuing right through the Dirty Thirties and up until funding for the Shrine of Democracy gave way to financial support for the Arsenal of Democracy leading up to World War II.

When the final ledger was tallied, Mount Rushmore cost just under $1 million to complete—or less than the price of paving a mile of highway today. While private contributions from corporations, philanthropic individuals, and even pennies from schoolchildren assisted in funding the early stages of the carving, federal appropriations to the project totaled $836,000.

While Mount Rushmore began as the dream of a scholarly historian, it was Borglum's artistic skills, drive, and dream to leave a lasting memorial that led to its fruition, firmly establishing him as a South Dakota legend. But lack of funding and US entry into World War II prevented Borglum's entire dream from ever being realized.

The sculptor's vision for Mount Rushmore did not fade away with the four faces of freedom visitors see today. Borglum's concept included a giant entablature to the side of the presidents, describing the nine most significant events in US history between 1776 and 1906, and an eight-hundred-step Grand Stairway that would lead to a narrow canyon directly behind the heads, where his crews would carve a large Hall of Records to protect the nation's most treasured artifacts. Fearing he would leave a mystery for the ages about why four giant granite portraits graced a remote mountain in the middle of the continent, as envisioned the impregnable hall also would have contained a record of western civilization and the importance of the four individuals depicted.

While the entablature concept was abandoned when the presidential portraits took up more room on the mountain than originally thought, Borglum did not immediately nix the plan for the Grand Stairway or the Hall of Records.

To that end, Borglum assigned a crew to carve the Hall of Records in the summer of 1938. By the middle of 1939, they had drilled, blasted, and excavated a sixty-eight-foot-deep, twenty-foot-high, twelve-foot-wide cavern. But with diminishing funds and a nation threatened by a growing war in Europe, the federal government then overseeing the project ordered him to stop work on the hall and concentrate on the faces.

Although Borglum died March 6, 1941, and never saw his plan for the grand hall realized, members of his family, including daughter Mary Ellis Borglum Vhay, and his grandchildren, carried the vision forward and saw the essence of his vision realized. On August 9, 1998, more than a half-century after the drills fell silent at Mount Rushmore, Vhay was joined by family members, National Park Service personnel, and members of the Mount Rushmore Society as a teakwood box, inserted in a titanium vault, was lowered into a small cavern carved in the floor of the entry to the Hall of Records, then covered by a granite capstone.

In the darkness of that teakwood box stand sixteen porcelain enamel panels inscribed with the story of Mount Rushmore and how it came to be carved, the reasons the four presidents were selected, and a brief history of the United States of America. Appropriately, a lone panel also describes the determined artist, statesman, and son of Danish immigrants, and the ragtag crew of drill-dusty miners he guided in creating one of the wonders of the world.

Chapter 14

"Jackson"—Deadwood's Mystery Man

On a sunny fall day in 2016, as a gentle breeze combed through the pine boughs towering above the silent gravesites of countless miners, muleskinners, merchants, and madams in Deadwood's fabled Mt. Moriah Cemetery, 160-year-old "Jackson," one of the town's original pioneers, was laid to rest.

Jackson's story is one of history and mystery, of a man in his mid-twenties who had joined a flood of fortune-seekers in Deadwood's earliest muddy and bloody years. While the cause of Jackson's demise may never be known, much has been learned since his skeletal remains were unearthed by a construction crew working on a retaining wall project in the spring of 2012.

The gruesome discovery that day in March 2012, nearly 140 years after the man was buried with dignity and a measure of ceremony, set off a two-year investigation involving the latest in forensic science, a study worthy of any CSI television drama. The probe's mission was quite simple: to unravel the identity of a pioneer prospector released from his mortal coil so long ago and buried in a forgotten grave situated in what would become the center of Deadwood's prestigious Presidential Neighborhood.

Historic preservation officials quickly surmised that Jackson had originally been buried in Ingleside, the town's first cemetery, near what would become the intersection of Taylor and Jackson Streets. Historical records indicate the interment had occurred between Deadwood's earliest origins in 1876 and the latter part of 1878.

State archaeologists and city personnel, assisted by a local archaeologist, carefully sifted through the site, collecting bone fragments and the remnants of a cranium. They found 99 percent of his skeleton, save for one tooth and a few small finger and toe bones.

Katie Lamie, an archaeologist with the South Dakota Archaeological Research Center, said she first met the deceased during that "dig" in March 2012, while she was monitoring the retaining wall project near the site of Wild Bill Hickok's original grave. She said Jackson had been "missed" several times before when previous construction projects had come just inches from his remains.

"None of the 100 or so other burials recovered from Deadwood's first cemetery between the years of 1878 and 2007, have been the subject of such archeological and scientific scrutiny," Lamie later noted. "Through the final episode of his life, this individual was apparently revered by a close group of friends or family."

Lamie noted that evidence recovered at the gravesite indicated that, at the time of his burial, the deceased had been well dressed in a coat and possibly a vest and shirt. Most notably, mourners at Jackson's original graveside service must have fired a three-round salute, as three spent .50–.70 center-fire cartridge cases were later found in his coat pockets.

The gruesome discovery set off a search for the mystery man's origins and identity using modern-day forensic techniques and enlisting the assistance of scientists and researchers from Georgia to Texas and Colorado to California. In the ensuing months, the Deadwood Historic Preservation Commission, backed by the Deadwood City Commission, invested thousands of dollars in scientific analysis of the skeletal remains.

That spring, Deadwood Dental's Dr. Lennard Hopper took digital x-rays of the teeth and jawbone of the remains he has labeled "Jackson" in his files, for the nearby street where the remains were found.

"We did a full mouth series of x-rays on the jaw segments, which were surprisingly intact," Hopper said. "The biggest challenge was positioning the sensors. A live patient can hold the x-ray sensor in position. Of course, that's not the case with skeletal remains."

Hopper said he spent a couple of hours taking individual x-rays of each tooth, as well as panoramic images showing the mandible.

"I never have done this before and it's another piece of Deadwood history," the dentist said. "The most fascinating thing I saw was some of the same dental materials and techniques that we use today."

Those x-rays were sent to forensic dentist Thomas David of Atlanta, whose subsequent report revealed the man was a habitual tobacco user and that he chewed on his right side, based on the wear on his teeth.

"That little piece right there, based on this one report, allows us to put a plug of tobacco in his right cheek," said Deadwood archivist Michael Runge. "That little piece of evidence adds to the all-encompassing look of who this individual really was."

In addition, David's $2,500 analysis of the deceased man's nine fillings, three of which were gold, revealed that "Jackson" had undergone multiple dental procedures by at least two different dentists, Runge explained. He also noted that in the late nineteenth century, most individuals would have simply had a bothersome tooth extracted, indicating the pioneering prospector was likely a man of some means.

"The gold leaf we saw on the fillings would have been done by someone with high expertise," David reported. "Later procedures were done by someone else with less experience."

Significantly, David also observed that "Jackson" did not hail from the East Coast as researchers originally surmised. His analysis showed fluorosis in the man's teeth, a condition commonly known as "Colorado brown stain," caused by natural fluoride levels in the water consumed by an individual at an early age, Runge said.

"When you're an infant to when you develop your adult teeth, the water you consume contains oxygen isotopes," Runge said. "Those oxygen isotopes adhere to your teeth and are distinctive to the region where you were born and raised. Colorado brown stain is found in the region from Texas to Nebraska, but not in Dakota Territory."

Early on, Diane France, a forensic anthropologist affiliated with the Human Identification Laboratory of Colorado in Fort Collins, began her study of the remains. A year after discovery of the remains, she concluded the man was five-foot-four to five-foot-eight, white, and eighteen to twenty-four years of age at the time of his death.

Tests by Dr. Angie Ambers, a DNA analyst and forensic geneticist with the Institute of Applied Genetics in Fort Worth, Texas, found that the man, who (she also surmises) probably died in his late teens or early twenties, likely had light red hair and light brown eyes and came from Western Europe.

"The DNA testing pointed out that this individual likely came from Western Europe—possibly Ireland, western England, or the coastal region of France," Runge said midway through the lengthy probe. "It's just another piece of the puzzle. We have multiple tests being performed on this individual."

"The man had nine fillings, six with silver tint amalgam and three that were gold, a rarity in the late 1800s," Runge explained. Further testing of the silver and gold extracted from the teeth will likely yield additional clues, he said.

"Testing will help us determine where the gold came from, as gold has its own unique signature and molecular composition," Runge said. "Gold throughout the world varies slightly on a molecular level, so we might be able to determine where this gold came from. It would be pretty amazing if this person had gold filling that came from the Black Hills.

"The spectral analysis will tell us what the amalgam was made from, what the percentages of tin, silver and mercury were used, and where the gold originated," Runge added. "It will tell us if it's Black Hills gold or if the gold came from Africa, South America, or Europe." A molecular analysis of the silver and gold extracted from the teeth, later conducted by the South Dakota School of Mines and Technology in an attempt to trace its origins, was inconclusive, Deadwood's historic preservation officer Kevin Kuchenbecker later reported.

Ambers completed a DNA analysis, allowing researchers to begin putting "a face" on the man who died of unknown causes in Deadwood's earliest days. Her work helped predict the man's hair, eye, and skin color, revealing details that local historic preservation officials could not possibly ascertain, Runge said.

When results of all the scientific inquiries were pooled with casts made of the man's mandible and cranium, the results were handed off to Austin-based forensic artist Karen Taylor, the woman charged with preparing a facial reconstruction for the project. Taylor's work ultimately took the skeletal remains from a bundle of bones to skin, Runge said.

"The result of this project will be to have the forensic artist put a face on this individual," he said. "All of the reports and tests we are performing on this individual—the DNA, isotopic and spectral analyses—will help her do her magic on the artwork and create a rendering of what this man would have looked like.

"What we're doing is taking the skeletal remains and piecing together the life of a man who lived 140 years ago," Runge said. "We're using modern forensic technologies to help piece together the life of this individual."

As the investigation came to a close, Kuchenbecker marveled at how many trained scientists and doctors had been involved in the probe, and how much they had learned. "With the DNA testing, looking at Y chromosomes, and a variety of other factors, we've

"JACKSON"—DEADWOOD'S MYSTERY MAN

been able to gain a sense of this individual," he said. "At this point, Jackson has probably traveled as much as anyone in this office. As a preservationist and an historian, it's been somewhat surprising that we can take a skeleton of a man who died about 140 years ago and learn so much about him."

The vast majority of investigative activities tied to the discovery of Jackson's remains came to an end with his reburial September 29, 2016, in the highest reaches of Mt. Moriah Cemetery. In so many senses it was, finally, the end of the trail for the young man who ventured to the American West lured by the color of gold.

While forensic investigators were unable to name the man or identify the cause of his death, several speakers at the small service said they had learned a great deal about the pioneer prospector who came to Deadwood Gulch in search of riches, only to breathe his last breath.

"Dead men do tell tales," said Dr. Ambers. "In this case, this young pioneer told us part of his story through his DNA and his skeletal remains. DNA is in a sense stardust, from a time that has passed."

She said no one could ever know the full story, except that the man's journey ended in Deadwood.

"The long-forgotten dead are longing for home," she said in goodbye.

Wild West re-enactors, looking the part in black frock coats, cowboy boots, and period dress, carried Jackson in a small redwood box built by a local craftsman to his new home, where he was re-interred just below the gravesite of Seth Bullock, the town's first marshal. A small marble marker denoted an "Unknown Pioneer" discovered in 2012 at the site of the city's first cemetery.

According to the priest who officiated at the services, Jackson was placed in an honored spot reserved for a young man who traveled west to find his fortune and who typified the pursuits of thousands of faceless pioneers, some of whom got rich while others died.

"This is actual history, not the Hollywood version," said Reverend Michael Johnson of Deadwood's St. John's Episcopal Church, the oldest church in the Black Hills. The priest, who wore vestments appropriate to an Episcopal priest of 1879, and recited from a 1789 book of common prayers, said the young man he helped bury was symbolic of the spirit of the American West.

"Jackson represents all of those long-forgotten people, a past that's still speaking to us," he said. "They came west to make it rich, but for some, that was the end of their story."

Bibliography

CHAPTER 1: WHERE THE BIG BOYS ARE BURIED

Griffith, T. D. and Dustin D. Floyd. *South Dakota's Black Hills and Badlands*, Fourth Edition. Guilford, CT: Globe Pequot Press, 2007.

Griffith, T. D. *South Dakota*. New York: Compass American Guides/Fodor's Travel Publications, 2004.

Author interviews with the late Dr. Larry Agenbroad, Dr. Jim Mead, former COO Joe Muller and Public Relations Coordinator Bethany Cook.

The Mammoth Site of Hot Springs, SD, Inc. www.mammothsite.org, accessed August 1, 2019.

CHAPTER 2: THE GHOST OF SETH BULLOCK, DEADWOOD'S FIRST LAWMAN

The Historic Bullock Hotel. www.historicbullock.com.

Chicago Tribune, February 24, 1903.

Parker, Watson. *Deadwood: The Golden Years.* Lincoln: University of Nebraska Press, 1981.

Griffith, T. D. Interviews of staff and guests, Bullock Hotel, Deadwood, SD; 1998–2018.

CHAPTER 3: PREACHER SMITH'S EARLY DEMISE

"Adams Museum." Deadwood History Inc. www.deadwoodhistory.com/about-us/properties/adams-museum.html, accessed August 1, 2019.

"Preacher Smith of Deadwood: Henry Weston Smith." Blackhillsvisitor.com. https://blackhillsvisitor.com/learn/preacher-smith-of-deadwood/, accessed August 1, 2019.

Lee, Bob. *The Black Hills After Custer.* Virginia Beach, VA: Donning Publishers, 1997.

McClintock, John S. *Pioneer Days in the Black Hills.* Norman: University of Oklahoma Press, 1939.

Parker, Watson. *Deadwood: The Golden Years.* Lincoln: University of Nebraska Press, 1981.

Rapid City Journal, November 3, 2009.

CHAPTER 4: DID DEADWOOD'S BROTHELS SPAWN THE TERM "CATHOUSE"?

Bryant, Jerry L., and Barbara Fifer. *Deadwood Saints and Sinners.* Helena, MT: Farcountry Press, 2016.

Floyd, Dustin D. "Busted! Can Black Hills Myths Take the Heat?" *Deadwood Magazine,* April 2006.

Parker, Watson. *Deadwood: The Golden Years*. Lincoln: University of Nebraska Press, 1981.

Chapter 5: Crazy Horse: Our Strange Man

Crazy Horse Memorial. Crazyhorsememorial.org, accessed August 1, 2019.

DeWall, Robb. *Crazy Horse and Korczak*. Crazy Horse, SD: Korczak's Heritage Inc., 1982.

McMurtry, Larry. *Crazy Horse*. New York: Penguin Putnam Inc., 1999.

Sandoz, Mari. *Crazy Horse: The Strange Man of the Oglalas*. New York: Hastings House, 1942.

Chapter 6: The Thoen Stone—Fact or Fraud?

Conradt, Stacy. *The Mystery of the Thoen Stone*. Mentalfloss.com, March 14, 2016. http://mentalfloss.com/article/76827/mystery-thoen-stone, accessed August 1, 2019.

Mischak, Jessica. "Images of the Past: The Thoen Stone." South Dakota Public Broadcasting, October 29, 2015. www.sdpb.org/blogs/images-of-the-past/the-thoen-stone/, accessed August 1, 2019.

Nolting, M. Timothy. "Across the Fence: Black Hills Gold and the Thoen Stone." *Sidney* [NE] *Sun-Telegraph*, June 29, 2013.

Thomson, Frank. *The Thoen Stone: A Saga of the Black Hills*. Oklahoma City: Harlo, 1966.

Chapter 7: Lame Johnny and the Lost Gold

Griffith, Tom. *Outlaw Tales of South Dakota*. Helena, MT: TwoDot Books, 2008.

Hasselstrom, Linda M. *Roadside History of South Dakota*. Helena, MT: Mountain Press Publishing, 1994.

Lawton, R. T. "Necktie Party Ended Lame Outlaw's Career." *Deadwood Magazine*, 2002.

Parker, Watson. *Deadwood: The Golden Years*. Lincoln: University of Nebraska Press, 1981.

Sinclair, Kelsey. "The Legend of Lame Johnny's Lost Gold." BHVisitor. https://blackhillsvisitor.com/learn/the-search-for-lame-johnnys-lost-treasure/, accessed August 1, 2019.

Chapter 8: Chief Two Sticks's Departure

Carr, G. Sam. "Sioux Chief Two Sticks." *Wild West Magazine*, June 2001.

Giago, Tim. "The Execution of Chief Comes Out Holy Two Sticks." *Native Sun News*, July 6, 2009.

Griffith, Tom. *Outlaw Tales of South Dakota*. Helena, MT: TwoDot Books, 2008.

Parker, Watson. *Deadwood: The Golden Years*. Lincoln: University of Nebraska Press, 1981.

Chapter 9: The Ghost of W. E. Adams

"Adams Museum." Deadwood History. https://www.deadwoodhistory.com/about-us/properties/adams-museum.html, accessed August 1, 2019.

"Adams House." HauntedHouses.com. https://ghost.hauntedhouses.com/south_dakota_deadwood_adams_house, accessed August 1, 2019.

Kopco, Mary. July 2019 interview with former executive director of the Adams Museum, Deadwood, SD.

Parker, Watson. *Deadwood: The Golden Years*. Lincoln: University of Nebraska Press, 1981.

Swisher, Kaija. "The Great Fire of Deadwood." *Black Hills Pioneer*, April 18, 2014.

"The Fire Fiend! Deadwood Destroyed." *Black Hills Daily Times*, November 4, 1879.

Chapter 10: The Underground Wilderness

Author's interviews with Wind Cave National Park Chief of Interpretation Tom Farrell, Jewel Cave National Park interpretive staff, and cave explorers: 1985—2019.

"Wind Cave National Park, South Dakota." National Park Service. www.nps.gov/wica, accessed August 1, 2019.

Chapter 11: An Unsolved Murder

Floyd, Dustin. "Deadwood's Dastardly Assassination." *Deadwood Magazine*, Deadwood, SD, March 2006.

Velder, Tim. "Surveyor Donates Map to Deadwood." *Rapid City Journal*, Rapid City, SD, October 21, 2003.

Author interviews with Kevin Kuchenbecker, Historic Preservation Officer, and Mike Runge, Archivist, City of Deadwood, South Dakota, May 2019.

Chapter 12: The Jackalope: South Dakota's Scariest Rabbit

Geller, Prof. "Jackalope." Mythology.net, September 30, 2018. https://mythology.net/mythical-creatures/jackalope/, accessed August 1, 2019.

Griffith, T. D. *South Dakota*. New York: Compass American Guides/Fodor's Travel Publications, 2004.

Jemison, Micaela. "The World's Scariest Rabbit Lurks Inside the Smithsonian's Collection." *Smithsonian Insider*, October 31, 2014. https://insider.si.edu/2014/10/worlds-scariest-rabbit-lurks-within-smithsonians-collection/, accessed August 1, 2019.

Simon, Matt. "Fantastically Wrong: The Disturbing Reality That Spawned the Mythical Jackalope." *Wired*, April 4, 2014. www.wired.com/2014/05/fantastically-wrong-jackalope/, accessed August 1, 2019.

Weiser, Kate. "Jackalopes of Wyoming—Myth or Reality?" *Legends of America*, November 2018. www.legendsofamerica.com/wy-jackalope/, accessed August 22, 2019.

CHAPTER 13: GUTZON BORGLUM: ONE MAN'S MOUNTAIN

Griffith, T. D. *America's Shrine of Democracy*. Rapid City, SD: Mount Rushmore Society, 1990.

"Mount Rushmore National Monument South Dakota." National Park Service. nps.gov/moru, accessed August 1, 2019.

Smith, Rex Alan. *The Carving of Mount Rushmore*. New York: Abbeville Press, 1985.

CHAPTER 14: "JACKSON"—DEADWOOD'S MYSTERY MAN

Griffith, Tom. "Deadwood Continues to Dig for Answers in 19th Century Death." *Rapid City Journal*, Rapid City, SD, March 4, 2014.

———. "Putting a Face on the Past: Modern Scientists Unraveling a Historic Mystery." *Rapid City Journal*, Rapid City, SD, June 24, 2014.

———. "Sleuths One Clue Closer to Identifying Early Miner. *Rapid City Journal*, Rapid City, SD, January 10, 2015.

———. "How Science and History Paired Up to Define Deadwood Mystery Man." *Rapid City Journal*, Rapid City, SD, September 30, 2016.

INDEX

A

Adams, Alice Burnham, 90, 91, 94
Adams Block Building, 90, 96
Adams Bros. Wholesale Grocery and Pioneer Fruit Company, 90
Adams, Helen, 90, 94
Adams House, 91, 96, 97, 98
Adams, James (W. E.'s brother), 86, 89, 90
Adams, James (W. E.'s father), 85
Adams, Lucile, 90, 91
Adams, Mary Mastrovich Vicich, 95, 96, 97
Adams-Mastrovich Family Foundation, 99
Adams Museum, 53, 84, 96, 97
Adams, Sarah Ann, 85
Adams, William Emery (W. E.), 85, 89, 91, 92, 95, 96, 99, 110
Agenbroad, Larry, 2, 3, 4
Ambers, Angie, 141, 142, 143
American Express Company, 86
Anderson, Phil, 1, 2, 3
Arapahoe, 41
Avenue of Flags, 123

B

Bacon, Charles, 76
Badlands National Park, 122
Ball, Roy, 119
Banner Grocery Store, 86, 88
Barnett, Gene, 65
Battle of the Hundred-in-the-Hands, 42
Battle of the Little Big Horn, 20, 46, 73, 74
Battle of the Rosebud, 44, 45
Bear Butte, 46
Bella Union (brothel), 28
Belle Fourche, South Dakota, 13
Bennett, John, 76
Bertrand, Alex, 84
Bertrand, Michigan, 85
Big Horn Mountains, 43, 50, 70
Bismarck, North Dakota, 50, 70, 87
Black Buffalo Woman, 39, 41
Black Shawl, 40
Bonaparte, Napoleon, 128
Borglum, Gutzon, 110, 123, 124, 125, 126, 127, 128, 129, 130, 131, 132, 133, 134, 135
Boulder Canyon, 115
Bozeman Trail, 41

INDEX

Brave Heart, 72
Bridger, Jim, 123
Brown, George L., 76
Brown, Jesse, 66, 68
Brown, T., 52, 55
Brule, 39
Buffalo Gap, 66, 68
Bullock, Seth, 10, 11, 12, 13, 14, 15, 16, 17, 18, 24, 26, 143
Burns, James H., 72
Bush, Charles, 103
Bush, Joe, 76, 77

C

Campbell, Hugh, 65
Canary, Calamity Jane, 22, 26, 30
Canyon Springs Station, 65, 66
Carr, Annie, 32
Carr, G. Sam, 77
Castle Creek, 61
cats, 33
Chadron, Nebraska, 67
Chadron State College, 2
Cheyenne and Black Hills Stage Company, 62
Cheyenne (tribe), 41, 44, 46
Cheyenne, Wyoming, 21, 33, 44, 57, 60, 62, 63, 65, 72, 87, 107
Chicago, Burlington & Quincy Railroad, 112
Chief Henry Standing Bear, 48
China Mary, 83
Cleveland, Grover, 74, 80
Cody, Buffalo Bill, 74, 123
Comes Out Holy Two Sticks. *See* Two Sticks

Conard, Fred, 116
Conn, Herb, 105
Conn, Jan, 105
Converse County, 120
Cook, Bethany, 8
Coolidge, Calvin, 129, 131
Coolidge, Grace, 130
Crawford, Nebraska, 3
Crazy Horse, 37, 38, 39, 40, 41, 42, 43, 44, 46, 47, 48, 49, 73
Crazy Horse Memorial, 48
Crazy Steve (horse-thief), 11
Cricket (brothel), 28
Crook City, South Dakota, 20, 24
Crook, George, 44, 47
Crow, 44, 54
Crow Dog, 74
Cultural Heritage Center, 71
Curly. *See* Crazy Horse
Custer City, South Dakota, 21, 51, 60
Custer County, 61
Custer, George Armstrong, viii, 21, 43, 45, 46, 50, 51, 52, 54, 56, 71
Custer State Park, 129

D

Dakota Territory, 11, 21, 44, 60, 70, 71, 85, 86, 140
Davidson, Alexander, 35
David, Thomas, 139
Davis, Scott, 65, 66
Deadwood City Commission, 139
Deadwood City Hall, 114, 117
Deadwood Flouring Mill Co., 13
Deadwood Gulch, 21, 32, 51, 86, 143

Deadwood Historic Preservation Commission, 139
Deadwood Hose Company, 110
Deadwood, South Dakota, viii, 10, 11, 12, 13, 14, 15, 16, 18, 19, 20, 21, 22, 23, 24, 25, 26, 27, 28, 29, 30, 31, 32, 33, 34, 35, 36, 51, 53, 56, 58, 60, 64, 65, 67, 72, 73, 78, 79, 82, 84, 85, 86, 88, 89, 90, 91, 92, 93, 94, 95, 96, 97, 99, 107, 108, 109, 110, 111, 113, 114, 115, 117, 130, 137, 138, 142, 143, 144
Denver, Colorado, 6, 16, 35, 62, 63
Derosier House, 97
DeSmet, South Dakota, 72
Digmann, Father, 80, 83
Donahue, Cornelius, 59, 60, 61, 62, 63, 64, 66, 69
Douglas, Wyoming, 119

E
Egan, Thomas, 72
Eisendrath, Simon, 91
Ellington, Connecticut, 20
Empire Bakery, 87
Eureka Safe & Lock Company, 117

F
Fairbault, Minnesota, 85
Farrell, Tom, 101, 105
Fetterman Massacre, 42
First Eagle, 75, 77
Floyd, Dustin, 35, 36, 114, 115, 116, 117
Fort Abraham Lincoln, 50
Fort Collins, Colorado, 140
Fort Laramie Treaty, 43, 44, 50, 52, 70
Fort Meade, 76
Fort Phil Kearny, 41
Fort Robinson, 47
Fort Worth, Texas, 141
France, Diane, 140
Franklin, Harris, 91
Fredericks, Rudolph, 114, 116
Fremont, John Charles, 125
French Creek, 44
Friendship Tower, 16

G
Gardner, C. V., 21
Gem (brothel), 28, 29
Gentles, William, 48
Ghost Dance movement, 72, 73
Giago, Tim, 73
Gilmore, James, 72
Girard College, 59
gold rush, 10, 19, 25, 28, 54, 57, 108, 127
Grafe, Ernest, 50
Greasy Grass, 46, 73
Great Fire of 1879, 88
Green Front (brothel), 28
Grouard, Frank, 47

H
Hall of Records (Mount Rushmore), 135
Hanson, George, 1, 2
Harrison, Benjamin, 70
Hearst, George, 62, 109
Hearst, William Randolph, 109

INDEX

Hell Canyon, 103
Hermosa, South Dakota, 130
Herrick, Douglas, 119
Herrick, Ralph, 119
Hickok, Wild Bill, 11, 26, 27, 30, 35, 72, 107, 108, 138
Hicks, Jay, 72
Hill City, South Dakota, 34, 60
Hill, Gale, 65
His Horses Looking. *See* Crazy Horse
Holen, Steve, 6
Holloch Cave, 103
Hollow Wood, 75, 78
Homestake Gold Mine, 61, 63, 108, 109
Homestake Hose Company, 110
Hopper, Lennard, 139
Horsted, Paul, 50
Hot Springs, South Dakota, 1, 2, 3, 5, 7, 8
Howe, Frank, 112
Human Identification Laboratory, 140
Hump, 41
Humphrey's cattle ranch, 75
Hunkpapa Lakota, 73
Hurley, John. *See* Donahue, Cornelius

I

Illingworth, William, 51
Independence, Missouri, 54
Indian Crow, 52, 55
Ingleside Cemetery, 138
Institute of Applied Genetics, 141

J

jackalope, 118, 119, 120, 121, 122
"Jackson" (Deadwood pioneer), 137, 139, 140, 144
Jefferson, Thomas, 123, 128
Jenney Stockade, 66
Jensen and Bliss Hardware Store, 87
Jewel Cave National Monument, 101, 103, 105, 106
Johnson, Michael, 144
Joslin, Lydia Ann, 20

K

Kelly, William, 76
Kent, R., 52, 54, 55
Kills the Two, 75, 77, 78
Kind, Ezra, 52, 54
King, William, 52, 55
Kopco, Alex, 97
Kopco, Mary, 91, 92, 97, 98
Kopco, Paul, 97
Kuchenbecker, Kevin, 142

L

LaBonte Hotel, 119
Lake, R. C., 88
Lakota, vii, viii, 37, 38, 40, 41, 44, 46, 47, 48, 50, 61, 70, 73, 74, 77, 79, 83, 84
Lame Johnny. *See* Donahue, Cornelius
Lamie, Katie, 138
Langrishe Theatre, 87
Larrabee, Nellie, 40
Lawrence County, 57, 80, 111

Lawrence County Recorder's Offices, 87
Lead, South Dakota, 60, 61, 65, 95, 108
Leehman, James, 72
Lewis and Clark, 123
Lincoln, Abraham, 123, 128
Lincoln, Robert Todd, 128
Little Big Man, 48
Little Hawk, 41
Lone Bear, 41
Lookout Mountain, 51
Louisiana Purchase, 128

M

Madison Aquifer, 106
Mahan, Shannon A., 6
Major Whitehead Expedition, 86
Mammoth Cave, 103
Mammoth Site, The, 2, 3, 4, 5, 6, 7, 8, 9
Matthiessen, Chris, 78
May, Boone, 66, 68
McCall, Crooked Nose Jack, 11, 72, 107
McKinley, William, 13
McLaughlin, "Big Nose", 65
McLaughlin, W. L., 80
McMurtry, Larry, 38, 40, 41, 44, 47
Meade County, 72
Mead, Jim, 3, 4, 6, 7
Melodean (brothel), 28
Michaud, Albert, 103
Michaud, Frank, 103
Miner, William, 65

Minneapolis, Minnesota, 86
Missouri River, 43, 50, 70, 71
Monitor (stagecoach), 62, 63, 64, 65, 69
Mount Roosevelt, 16
Mount Rushmore National Memorial, vii, 48, 110, 123, 126, 128, 129, 130, 131, 133, 134, 135
Mount Rushmore National Memorial Society, 129
Mt. Moriah Cemetery, 137, 143
Muller, Joe, 8
Murphy, John, 60

N

National Museum of Natural History, 118
Native American Journalists Association, 73
News and Pioneer, 87
Nodaway, Missouri, 109
Nolting, M. Timothy, 54
Norbeck, Peter, 124, 129
No Water, 39, 75
No Waters, 76, 77, 78

O

Oglala, 37, 39, 73
Oglala Lakota, 73
Optimisticeskaja Cave, 103
Oregon Trail, 41
Oslund, Pete, 68
Overland Hotel, 87
Ovid, Idaho, 125

INDEX

P

Panama Canal, 129
Parker, Watson, 13, 22, 23, 29, 30, 57, 58, 64
Pasadena, California, 91, 95
Peck, Frank, 109, 110, 111, 112, 113, 114, 115, 116, 117
Peck, Martha Baxter, 109, 111
Peemiller, Marshal, 80
Pence, James, 112
Philadelphia, Pennsylvania, 59
Pierre, South Dakota, 87
Pine Ridge Agency, 75, 77
Pine Ridge Indian Reservation, 67
Presidential Neighborhood (Deadwood), 138

R

Rapid City, South Dakota, vii, 125
rats and mice (in brothels), 32
Red Cloud Agency, 47, 61
Remer, William, 84, 117
Robinson, Doane, 124
Rodin, Auguste, 125
Roosevelt, Theodore, 10, 11, 12, 13, 14, 15, 16, 101, 102, 103, 123, 128, 129, 131, 132
Rosebud Valley, 44
Royce, R., 76
Runge, Michael, 140, 141, 142
Rushmore, Charles E., 127

S

Sacagawea, 123
Sample, Bill, 66

Sandoz, Mari, 41, 47
Santa Fe, New Mexico, 54
Savannah, Missouri, 109
Seth's Cellar (bar), 16
Sexton, Inez, 29
Sherman, William Tecumseh, 41, 43
Shoshone, 44
Sidney, 87
Sioux, 41, 43, 52
Sioux Falls, South Dakota, 72
Sitting Bull, 43, 46, 73, 74, 75
Smith, Frank "Whispering", 67
Smith, Henry Weston, 19, 20, 21, 22, 24, 25, 26, 27
Smith, Rex Alan, vii
Society of Black Hills Pioneers, 26
South Dakota Archaeological Research Center, 138
South Dakota School of Mines and Technology, 142
South Dakota State Historical Society, 124
Spearfish, South Dakota, 51, 53, 87, 110
Spotted Tail Agency, 48
Standing Rock Reservation, 74
Star, Sol, 11, 13, 14
State Game Lodge, 130
Statuary Hall (US Capitol), 125
St. John's Episcopal Church, 144
St. Joseph's Hospital, 112
Stone Mountain Confederate Memorial Association, 125
Stone Mountain, Georgia, 124
Sturgis, South Dakota, 46, 72, 76

Sully County, 72
Swearengen, Al, 29, 31

T
Taft, William Howard, 13
The 400 (club), 32
They-Are-Afraid-of-Her, 41
Thoen, Ivan, 51, 53
Thoen, Louis, 51, 52, 53, 56
Thoen Stone, 52, 53, 54, 55, 56
Thompson, Nathaniel, 72
Thompson, Phatty, 33, 34, 36
Thomson, Frank, 53
Thorpe, Doc, 112
Thunderhead Mountain, 49
Two Sticks, 73, 74, 75, 76, 77, 78, 79, 80, 81, 82, 83, 84

U
Unsolved Mysteries (television program), 16
Uses a Fight, 75, 79
Utter, Colorado Charlie, 35

V
Vhay, Mary Ellis Borglum, 135

W
Wall Drug Store, 122
Washington, DC, 14, 127
Washington, George, 123, 128
Whiteface Horses, 75, 77, 78, 79
White River, 75
Wilson, Woodrow, 13
Wind Cave National Park, 101, 102, 103, 104, 106
Windy City Lake, 106
Women's Dress, 47
Wood, G. W., 52, 55
Worm (Crazy Horse's father), 39
Wounded Knee Creek, 74
Wounded Knee massacre, 72, 74

Y
Yankton, South Dakota, 70, 72, 108
Young Man Afraid of His Horses, 76, 77

Z
Ziolkowski, Korczak, 48
Ziolkowski, Ruth, 48

About the Author

Tom Griffith has been a reporter, photographer, and managing editor in Flagstaff, Arizona, Havre, Montana, and Rapid City, South Dakota. In a varied career, he served as the first employee of the Mount Rushmore Society, helping raise $25 million and stage the formal dedication of the memorial with President George H. W. Bush and actor Jimmy Stewart, among others, founded an advertising agency then sold it, and has written or co-authored more than seventy books for major publishers including Random House, Simon & Schuster, and Globe Pequot Press.

Tom's travel writing and photography has taken him to eighty countries and his features have appeared in more than three hundred newspapers and magazines from New York to New Zealand, including *Rolling Stone India*, *True West*, *Hadassah*, *Historic Traveler*, *Where to Retire*, *Volaris*, the *Chicago Tribune*, *Houston Chronicle*, *Denver Post*, the *Times of India*, and the *New Zealand Herald*. He also has been a columnist for *AAA Home & Away*.

A member of the prestigious Society of American Travel Writers, Tom served on the organization's national board of directors, representing more than a thousand of the most productive travel journalists and photographers in the nation, as well as chairman of its Central States Chapter. He remains an active member of SATW.

President Reagan wrote the foreword to Tom's first book, *America's Shrine of Democracy*, while NBC's Tom Brokaw wrote the foreword to his forty-fourth book, *A Winning Tradition*. His previous works for Globe Pequot Press have included *Outlaw Tales of South Dakota*, *Outlaw Tales of Nebraska*, *Deadwood: The Best Writing on the Most Notorious Town in the West*, and *The Insiders' Guide to South Dakota's Black Hills & Badlands*.

Tom and his wife, Nyla, who is a published novelist, live and write in the highest reaches of South Dakota's fabled Black Hills.

Made in the USA
Monee, IL
08 January 2024